Other books in the Survey Research Center's
Research Program in Religion and Society:

N. J. Demerath III, **Social Class in American Protestantism,**
(Chicago: Rand McNally, 1965)

Charles Y. Glock and Rodney Stark, **Religion and Society in Tension,** (Chicago: Rand McNally, 1965)

Charles Y. Glock and Rodney Stark, **Christian Beliefs and Anti-Semitism,** (New York: Harper and Row, 1966)

Donald Metz, **New Congregations: Security and Mission in Conflict,** (Philadelphia: Westminister Press, 1967)

Charles Y. Glock, Benjamin B. Ringer, and Earl R. Babbie, **To Comfort and To Challenge: A Dilemma of the Contemporary Church,** (Berkeley & Los Angeles: University of California Press, 1967)

PATTERNS OF RELIGIOUS COMMITMENT

VOLUME ONE

AMERICAN PIETY:

THE NATURE OF RELIGIOUS COMMITMENT

AMERICAN PIETY: THE NATURE OF RELIGIOUS COMMITMENT

by Rodney Stark and Charles Y. Glock

A publication from the Research
Program in Religion and Society
of the Survey Research Center,
University of California, Berkeley

1970 / Berkeley   Los Angeles   London
UNIVERSITY OF CALIFORNIA PRESS

University of California Press
Berkeley and Los Angeles, California

University of California Press, Ltd.
London, England

Copyright © 1968 by The Regents of the University of California
Library of Congress Catalog Card Number 68–12792

International Standard Book Numbers:
        Cloth: 0–520–01210–0
        Paper: 0–520–01756–0

Printed in the United States of America
Second Printing

PREFACE

Religion has lagged far behind other special topics in the social sciences primarily because of an almost total lack of research funds. While such topics as poverty, race relations, education, and politics have received large-scale research support from foundations and government, research by independent scholars on the role of religion in society has gone virtually unfunded. Government agencies have perhaps been fearful that support of such research would entangle them in problems of the separation of church and state. Private foundations, insofar as research on religion—rather than church action—is concerned, have been generally uninterested in the topic.

As a consequence, most of our small present store of empirical knowledge about religion has been obtained through fortuitous means. Much of this information has come through reanalysis of data originally collected for other purposes. However, even here research has been greatly stymied. The major source of data for social science reanalysis is provided by the United States Census. Indeed, a good many social scientists devote their careers to analyzing census data in order to increase our knowledge of how societies operate. Unfortunately, even the single question of religious affiliation is excluded from the census because of organized protests by minority religious bodies.[1] Thus census data are without utility for the study of religion. We hardly possess accurate information on the relative size of various religious bodies and we cannot study changes in their size during past decades.

[1] See the excellent discussion in William Peterson, "Religious Statistics in the United States," *Journal for the Scientific Study of Religion*, I, No. 2 (1962), pp. 165–178.

A second major source of data for secondary analysis is survey studies. However, while most surveys inquire about politics, social class, and the like, they rarely ask anything more about religion other than whether persons are Protestants, Catholics, or Jews (when they ask that). Thus, data for secondary analysis to enlighten us upon the social role of religion have been very meager, available only through occasional happenstance.

Furthermore, even most of the original studies devoted to learning about religion have occurred rather fortuitously. The most important original study in recent years, Gerhard Lenski's, *The Religious Factor*,[2] was only possible because the University of Michigan conducts a Detroit Area Study each year as a device for student training. The faculty member who teaches research methods to first-year graduate students in a given year has the option of using the survey to pursue his own interests. Thus, the first significant body of empirical data on religion in many decades of empirical social research activities was obtained simply because a professor interested in the sociology of religion directed the Detroit Area Study one year. Although Professor Lenski did receive several small grants to support him while he wrote his book and to pay for secretarial aid, it is unlikely that he could have found funds to conduct the survey through means other than those which a student training program provided him.

A potentially major source of support for the scientific study of religion is, obviously, the churches themselves. For clearly they have a crucial stake in determining the present nature of religion in our society. But so far the churches have not provided significant funding. They do spend large sums each year on social science studies and surveys, but these are nearly always conducted by their own employees. Sad to say, virtually nothing of merit has come from these internal research enterprises. One reason is that these studies are typically devoted to extremely applied questions. As is usually the case in science, applied work is sterile when it is not guided by an adequate corpus of basic research.

These remarks on the economics of research on religion are intended to illuminate the complicated funding of the present

[2] Garden City, N.Y.: Doubleday, 1961.

study. Large-scale social research is relatively expensive, and our study is no exception. However, during much of its duration it was done with virtually no direct support. The study was made possible initially by a convergence of our interests in religion and the interest of the Anti-Defamation League of B'nai B'rith in the effects of religion on contemporary anti-Semitism. In collecting the empirical data necessary for a study of religion and anti-Semitism it was possible to collect a major array of data on religious beliefs and behavior. Having discharged our obligations to the A.D.L. by completing the anti-Semitism study,[3] we were left in possession of the data on which these three volumes are based.

However, we still needed considerable money to pay for computer time and other data processing services, for clerical assistance, and to support the authors during the analysis and writing. In contrast to the costs of doing such an investigation from scratch, these were relatively small amounts. The data, including both national and regional samples, cost several hundred thousand dollars to collect. We began by seeking $30,000 with which to exploit this windfall of potential knowledge.

Then came several fruitless rounds of proposals to foundations, government agencies, and denominational headquarters. While we received a great deal of encouragement, we received little money. Indeed, had it not been for the good offices of Yoshio Fukuyama, then director of research of the United Church of Christ, we would have received none. We wish to express our deepest gratitude to the United Church of Christ for a grant of $1,500 which at the time made the difference between being able to continue or not. Thus the first book was completed, financed for the most part through the old army technique of "scrounging." Of course if the original costs of collecting the survey data had not already been paid for, the study would have been absolutely impossible. Consequently, we are extremely indebted to the A.D.L. for providing the funds for the original data collection. Indeed, the A.D.L. was a most generous and sympathetic sponsor of our research, and its program director, Mr.

[3] Charles Y. Glock and Rodney Stark, *Christian Beliefs and Anti-Semitism* (New York and London: Harper and Row, 1966).

Oscar Cohen, greatly encouraged and aided the present study even though it was not related to the A.D.L.'s concerns.

But even scrounging has practical limits. As we turned to Volumes Two and Three of the study we began to doubt seriously our ability to write them without some substantial funding. But like a good old-fashioned melodrama it all came right in the end. A proposal submitted to the National Science Foundation (GS-1592) was approved in April, 1967, providing adequate funds to support completion of the last two volumes of the study.[4]

If at times we lacked research funds, at no time did we lack intellectual aid and support. We would like to acknowledge the contributions made to this study by our colleagues who participate in the Survey Research Center's Research Program in Religion and Society. These include Earl R. Babbie, Stephen Steinberg, Gertrude Jaeger Selznick, Armand Maas, Donald Metz, and Sister Ruth Wallace. Other colleagues at the center also made thoughtful criticisms of our work, including Travis Hirschi, Shannon Ferguson, William L. Nicholls II, and Robert E. Mitchell. We would also like to thank John Lofland, Jeffrey K. Hadden, Jay Demerath, Langdon Gilkey, Andrew J. Greeley, Phillip E. Hammond, Benton Johnson, Gerhard Lenski, Martin E. Marty, James A. Pike, David Riesman, Guy E. Swanson, and Milton Yinger. Miss Antoinette Brown spared us a great deal of effort and responsibility by managing all of the computer work.

R.S.
C.Y.G.

Berkeley, California

[4] It must be emphasized that the National Science Foundation is in no way responsible for the views expressed in this study and exercises no editorial control over the content of reports written with its financial support.

CONTENTS

INTRODUCTION

Both organizationally and theologically, the heart of religion is commitment. Historically, the primary concern of all religious institutions has been to lead men to faith, and the continued existence of any religion would seem to depend upon accomplishing this task.

Despite the primacy of this aspect of religion, it has been little studied. Virtually no systematic attempts have been made to determine what factors contribute to or inhibit the efforts of religious institutions to recruit and maintain a committed membership.[1] Consequently, while a good deal is known about social and psychological influences on voting, or the purchase of consumer goods, little or nothing is known about why some men are earnest in their religious faith and practice, while others are indifferent or even hostile to religion. Considering the lip service social scientists give to the premise that religion is one of the most important social institutions, this prevailing ignorance seems a major impediment to constructing any systematic science of society.

A second equally crucial question about religious commitment has gone as nearly unexplored: What difference does religious commitment make? What are the consequences in the lives of men of a deeply-felt faith? Does it make them happier, more charitable, more honest, better citizens? Does religious commitment have pernicious results? While scholars have been interested in the effects of religious commitment for a long time, efforts to find empirical answers to these questions have been few. Furthermore, even those studies that have been conducted are vitiated by

---

[1] Recently, Michael Argyle has attempted a systematic summary of all available studies and empirical data bearing on the socio-psychological sources of religious commitment. Even in such creative and competent hands as his, the poverty of our knowledge in this area resulted in a book that was very slim both quantitatively and qualitatively. See: *Religious Behaviour* (Glencoe, Ill.: The Free Press, 1959).

very primitive notions of the meaning of religious commitment. Typically, studies of the effects of religion have not considered differences in the *degree* to which persons are committed to religion. Instead they have mainly concentrated on simple comparisons between Protestants and Catholics. In the very few instances when studies have sought the effects of *variations* in religious commitment, this has usually meant no more than examining differences between regular and irregular church attenders.[2] Thus, not only has there been a paucity of research of any kind on religious behavior, but the unsophisticated quality of most of the research that has been done has further exacerbated the religious "knowledge gap."

This state of the field both provides opportunities and imposes burdens upon the present study. Because so little has been done previously we have the opportunity of working with the first relatively comprehensive body of empirical data on religious behavior. Thus, in terms of sheer description and empirical generalization we can hardly fail to make some important contributions. Much theoretical effort has been wasted too often in trying to account for a state of affairs believed to exist, but which in fact did not. If one knows no more than that something is empirically the case it at least provides a fruitful basis for speculation about why this is so. However, we are also faced with the burden of taking up the quest to understand religious behavior virtually de

[2] The most widely hailed study of the effects of religious commitment is Gerhard Lenski's, *The Religious Factor* (Garden City, N.Y.: Doubleday, 1961). While it is true that Lenski devotes considerable attention early in his book to discussing a variety of ways of assessing religious commitment, when it comes to analyzing the consequences of religion he rarely uses any of these measures of commitment because the small size of his sample made it nearly impossible to do so. Instead, his "religious factor" usually consists of the nominal categories Protestant, Catholic, and Jew (with Protestants separated into whites and Negroes). Thus, Lenski does not provide any real enlightenment about the effects of religious commitment, but simply looks for differences among persons who identify themselves with one of the three main religious groupings. Consequently, it is never at all clear what the differences Lenski reports might be attributed to—do they stem from differences in religious ideology, in ethnicity, or what? We shall have occasion frequently in Volume Three to discuss Lenski's findings and interpretations, and to try to discover what it is about religion, if anything, that accounts for them.

novo. For the most part we must formulate original theories, conceptual schemes, and empirical measures because no adequate body of previous work exists to be drawn upon.[3] Possibly this necessity has given birth to some modest invention.

The aim of the study, then, is to seek answers to three fundamental questions about religious commitment:

1. What is the nature of religious commitment?
2. What are the social and psychological sources of religious commitment?
3. What are the social and psychological consequences of religious commitment?

Our attempts to answer these questions are being reported in three volumes of which this is the first. Each volume may be read independently of the others. Still, the reader of any one volume will benefit from knowing what all three are about.

VOLUME ONE. AMERICAN PIETY:
THE NATURE OF RELIGIOUS COMMITMENT

In order to study what causes religious commitment or what effects it has on other aspects of human behavior, it is necessary first to decide just what religious commitment *is* and to select means for measuring it. The concept of religious commitment is extremely ambiguous—it means many different things to different men. In order to come to terms with this ambiguity all of the possible meanings of commitment have to be determined and the empirical relevance of these distinctions has to be assessed. These are essentially the tasks taken up in Volume One.

Thus, in Volume One we shall develop a linguistically comprehensive set of standards for religious commitment and then see the extent to which they are empirically independent. It is quite

[3] This is not to imply that there is no important theoretical heritage in the sociology of religion, for the monumental work of Max Weber, Emil Durkheim, and a host of nineteenth-century scholars constitutes an imposing legacy of theory. However, this work is mainly aimed at understanding macrocosmic aspects of religious institutions—the function and impact of religion at the level of society as a whole—and little has been written about religion at the level of individual behavior.

possible, for example, that several or all of these criteria of religious commitment are so empirically related that they are, for all practical purposes, the same thing. On the other hand, it may be that religious commitment defined in one way has rather little to do with commitment defined in another way. These questions necessarily must be resolved before other questions concerning religious commitment can be taken up.

In addition to trying to conceptualize and measure individual religious commitment, Volume One takes advantage of the descriptive opportunity provided by the data to explore the character of Christian denominationalism in modern America. It has recently become common to suggest that the days of denominationalism are virtually gone, that out of a schismatic past has arisen a unified, "common core" religion, and that the future holds a reunification of the faith. But somehow, when one looks beyond the superstructures, such as the Ecumenical Council, the National Council of Churches of Christ, or the ministerial associations, to such current religious phenomena as "God is Dead" theology on the one hand, and charges of heresy against an Episcopal bishop on the other, suspicion arises that we are far from a unified religious perspective. In Volume One these suspicions are investigated.

Volume One will also afford an occasion to ponder the future course of American religion. Will the church survive as we have known it, will it assume a radically different character in the future, or is it destined eventually for extinction? Virtually all observers agree that American religion is in a state of transition, but there is less agreement upon what this transition is exactly and where it may lead. Our own data do not provide the grounds for settling the debate. They can, however, clarify some of the central issues.

VOLUME TWO. THE POOR IN SPIRIT: SOURCES OF RELIGIOUS COMMITMENT

Having devoted Volume One to developing an understanding of what religious commitment is, Volume Two will explore the conditions under which it occurs. Who responds favorably to the call of religion, who is unmoved, and what accounts for the differences? We shall explore the effect of a wide range of social and psychological variables upon religious commitment, but special attention will be given to developing and testing a general theory of deprivation; in brief, that religious commitment results from the individual's failure to find satisfaction and reward from his participation in the larger society. However, in pursuing the quest to understand why some kinds of persons are more religious than others, comparisons will be required which are also of intrinsic descriptive interest. Thus, contrasting patterns and degrees of religious commitment will be examined for men and women, the old and the young, urbanites and rurals, whites and Negroes, among the various regions of the country, among the rich and the poor, the educated and uneducated.

VOLUME THREE. BY THEIR FRUITS: CONSEQUENCES OF RELIGIOUS COMMITMENT

To what extent do specifically religious influences matter in shaping the lives and behavior of modern Americans? In Volume Three we shall seek the intended and unintended consequences of religious commitment upon such things as social mobility, economic behavior, intellectualism and cultural sophistication, political choices and political ideology, civil libertarianism, and racial and religious prejudice. There has been considerable speculation that religious commitment affects each of these aspects of life, and some empirical research has been done in an effort to resolve a few of these questions. However, both the theoretical expectations and the empirical literature are filled with contradictions and ambiguities that demand resolution before we can say if and how religion does play a role in modern life.

Furthermore, all investigations of the consequences of religious commitment necessarily depend upon knowing something about its causes. Before a correlation between, for example, religious commitment and civil libertarianism can be asserted to be a consequence of religion it is necessary to show that religious commitment and civil libertarianism are not simply both the consequences of some other factor.

Thus, the degree to which it is possible to have any confidence in attributing some consequence to religion is in part determined by how accurately one knows the sources of religious commitment. For only to the degree that these sources are known can the proper controls for testing correlations between religious commitment and other behavior be applied.

To a great extent, then, our success in isolating sources of religious commitment in Volume Two will set limits on the adequacy of our search for the consequences of religious commitment in Volume Three. Of course, both Volumes Two and Three initially depend upon our satisfactorily coming to terms with what religious commitment *is* in Volume One. Thus the structure of the study is set by the logic underlying our investigation; each new question will be built upon what came before it.

DETAILS OF THE SURVEY

So far this introduction has been concerned with an overview of the aims to be pursued in these volumes. Something must be said now about the means that will be employed.

Two bodies of data will be drawn upon: an elaborate questionnaire study of church members in Northern California, and a national sample of adult Americans.

The church-member sample: Three thousand persons, randomly selected from the church member population of four Northern California counties (Marin, San Francisco, San Mateo, and Santa Clara), completed a lengthy and detailed questionnaire during the spring and summer of 1963. This questionnaire asked nearly 500 different questions concerning religious beliefs and practices, political attitudes and behavior, prejudice, leisure time use, and the like. The majority of respondents took great care in completing the questionnaire as evidenced by the richness of unsolicited comments written into the margins and covers, and even appended in the form of lengthy letters. Nearly half took the trouble to write lengthy additional comments.

This sample was obtained first by randomly selecting a sample of congregations, weighted for size, from all Protestant and Roman Catholic congregations in the four counties. After thus selecting ninety-seven Protestant congregations, and twenty-one Roman Catholic parishes, a random sample of members was obtained by sampling individual membership lists.[4]

A response rate of 72 percent among the Protestants and 53 percent among Roman Catholics was obtained by the questionnaire. Telephone interviews conducted with three hundred persons randomly selected from Protestant non-respondents and two hundred from among the Catholics showed the data satisfactorily represented the overall population sampled. A lengthy methodological appendix reporting the details of sampling and the representativeness of the data was included in the initial volume based on these data.[5] That volume also includes a reproduction of the questionnaire which was used.

The national sample: Eighteen months after the questionnaires were mailed to the church-member sample, some of the most important items were included in interviews conducted with a representative sample of the national adult population in October, 1964. In all, 1,976 persons were interviewed nationwide. Both sampling and interviewing were done by the National Opinion Research Center. Their techniques, developed through several decades of conducting nationwide surveys, are widely respected. A full account of the sampling methodology is reported in another volume based on these same national data.[6] However, it seems appropriate to report here one important test of the representativeness of the sample. Table 1 compares the proportions of persons in various religious bodies as estimated both by our national survey sample and by a survey conducted in 1957 by the United States

[4] Due to a failure of data collection among Negro congregations, and because virtually no Negroes were found in non-Negro congregations, the church-member sample is exclusively white.

[5] Charles Y. Glock and Rodney Stark, *Christian Beliefs and Anti-Semitism* (New York: Harper and Row, 1966).

[6] Gertrude Jaeger Selznick and Stephen Steinberg, *Anti-Semitism in America* (tentative title) (New York: Harper and Row, in press).

Table 1

THE REPRESENTATIVENESS OF THE SAMPLE

	United States Census Bureau Sample Survey * (1957)	Survey Research Center National Sample (1964)
Protestant	66.2%	68.1%
Baptist	19.7	19.3
Methodist	14.0	13.1
Lutheran	7.1	8.8
Presbyterian	5.6	5.8
Episcopal	⎫	2.9 ⎫
Congregational	⎬19.8	2.2 ⎬21.1
Other Protestant	⎭	16.0 ⎭
Roman Catholic	25.7	25.8
Jewish	3.2	3.1
Other non-Christian	1.3	0.5
None	2.7	2.5
Not reported	0.9	0.0
	100.0%	100.0%

* *U.S. Bureau of the Census, Current Population Reports, series P-20, no. 79* (Feb. 2, 1958).

Census Bureau.[7] The census survey was based on 25,000 cases and thus ought to be a very accurate estimate of actual religious distribution of the population. As can be seen in the table, our data very closely approximate the census study. Our data include a slightly greater proportion of Protestants, produced by the fact that we found slightly more Lutherans than did the census study,

[7] This survey was the first time the Census Bureau ever collected data on religious affiliation, and at the time it was hoped that this indicated such a question would be included in the 1960 census. However, because of vigorous complaints from a small number of persons and several organizations this was not done. Even more serious is the fact that following publication of a preliminary report of this survey study, from which these data were taken, the Census Bureau decided to suppress all further data from the survey. At the time this went to press nothing further had been released and scholars had been barred from access to the material. As William Petersen remarked, "I know of no other instance in its long and honorable record when data actually assembled by the Census Bureau were suppressed. This morally disturbing, and possibly even illegal, act would be inconceivable with respect to statistics on any other subject." *Journal for the Scientific Study of Religion,* I, No. 2 (1962), p. 173.

and a slightly lower proportion of persons belonging in the "other non-Christian" category. However, the discrepancies are trivial. The close correspondence between our findings and those of the census study lend considerable confidence to the representativeness of our sample.

The availability of the national sample will permit us to examine relationships explored in detail in the church-member sample to see if they apply to all regions of the country. In the volumes that follow these different bodies of data will be used in juxtaposition in order to exploit the relative advantages of each.

However, the national sample will not permit us to extend our investigation beyond Christianity. The church-member sample, of course, contains only Christians. While the national sample includes Jews, various other non-Christian faiths, and persons without any religious identification, their numbers are too small to permit study. This does not reflect a choice on our part to limit our investigation to Christians. We would very much prefer to have had adequate samples of Jews and other non-Christians and to have included them in our study. However, we lacked the funds to obtain them.

Having now provided an introductory statement of our general aims, and the means by which these will be pursued, we may turn once again to the present volume to provide a more detailed overview of its contents and the way it has been organized.

ORGANIZATION

Any examination of religious commitment must confront immediately the task of definition. This is basically the topic of Chapter 1 which conceives four principal ways in which religious commitment may be expressed: belief, practice, experience, and knowledge. These four dimensions of commitment are then examined separately and in detail in succeeding chapters.

Chapters 2 and 3 are focused on religious belief, Chapters 4 and 5 on religious practice, Chapter 6 on religious experience, and Chapter 7 on religious knowledge. In these chapters, the responses of American Christians to the questions which were designed to tap these different dimensions are first examined descriptively. Then the task of constructing and validating summary measures for each dimension (and where appropriate, its subparts) is confronted.

Chapter 8 examines the nature of the social relations among church members, the extent to which churches serve as primary groups.

Chapter 9 investigates the extent to which these measures are empirically independent, in effect, to discover how much expressing religious commitment in one way has to do with expressing it in another.

Chapter 10 considers changing patterns of denominational affiliation over time by studying shifts in such affiliations within and between generations.

Finally, Chapter 11 ponders the significance of what has been learned about American religion for the future of the church.

Chapter 1

THE NATURE
OF RELIGIOUS
COMMITMENT[1]

*Every definition
is dangerous.*
Erasmus

When we say someone is "religious" we can mean many different things. Church membership, belief in religious doctrines, an ethical way of life, attendance at worship services, and many other acts, outlooks and conditions can all denote piety and commitment to religion.

Upon reflection, it becomes clear that the variety of meanings associated with the term religious, while they may well be aspects of a single phenomenon, are not simply synonyms. For example, most people knowing that someone is an active church member would also expect him to be a firm believer in church doctrines and to be concerned about acting out his faith in his daily life. Going to church, believing, and acting ethically are generally recognized as components of being religious. However, simply because a person is religious in one of these ways is no guarantee that he will be religious in others. There are active church-goers who do not believe, firm believers among the unchurched, and people who both believe and belong, but who could hardly be described as ethical. Deciding with any particular precision who warrants the designation "religious" and who does not, turns out to be rather a complex problem.

The ambiguities in what religiousness can mean have led to serious failures in much research and writing on religious commitment. A good part of the recent dispute over whether American

[1] The basic conceptual scheme presented in this chapter is elaborated in greater detail in Charles Y. Glock and Rodney Stark, *Religion and Society in Tension* (Chicago: Rand McNally, 1965), ch. 2.

religion experienced a postwar revival or decline seems to have been produced by different observers adopting different definitions. While some commentators pointed to increases in the proportion of Americans belonging to and participating in churches, others detected an erosion of biblical faith and asserted that religion was losing its authenticity. Since it seems likely that both of these changes were occurring simultaneously, whether one discerned a religious revival or decline depended at least partly on whether religiousness was defined in terms of practice or belief.[2]

Clearly, conceptions of religiousness are not the same to all men—either in modern complex societies or even in the most homogeneous primitive communities. This simple fact scarcely needs documentation. The evidence that people disagree about how the "religious person" ought to think, feel, and act is all around us.

Because of this great diversity, any investigation of the individual and his religion faces a formidable problem of definition— what shall we call religiousness and how shall we decide to classify persons in religious terms? There are several issues at stake in this matter. First of all there is the purely methodological problem of selecting criteria that may be applied unambiguously and systematically. However, since science mainly operates with nominal definitions, from a purely methodological point of view we could arbitrarily define religious commitment pretty much as we cared to. Our subsequent statements and findings, however, would only be applicable to religious commitment in the particular sense in which we defined it. But of course we aspire to do a good deal more than that; we want to make statements that will be agreed to have general applicability. Thus we come to a second consideration in defining our terms. This has to do with credibility or perhaps relevance. In order to make assertions about religious commitment that will be regarded as relevant it is necessary that readers agree that the way we define religiousness suitably represents the way they understand the term. If we want to have our statements taken as applicable to what is conventionally

[2] An analysis of the religious revival controversy is treated in detail in Glock and Stark, *op. cit.*, chs. 4 and 5.

regarded as religious commitment then we must come to terms with conventional usage of the term religious commitment.

But, as we have just pointed out, the term religiousness is used in a number of different ways and is subject to a great deal of ambiguity in conventional usage. Thus, to begin the task of defining and operationalizing religious commitment it is necessary to do a bit of linguistic analysis to determine the different things that *can* be meant by the term, or the different ways in which individuals *can* be religious. Subsequently, it becomes appropriate to try to discover whether religiousness manifested in one of these ways has anything to do with its being expressed in others.

The discussion which follows presents our attempt to provide a linguistically comprehensive set of criteria of religious commitment. Subsequent chapters will take up each of these criteria in detail and propose and test strategies for measuring each. Later, in Chapter 9 we will come back to an assessment of the problem of definition. Having begun with all the possible distinctions in what religiousness can mean, we shall see whether such distinctions are empirically necessary. In real life are people who are religious in one way also religious in other ways, or are the various ways of expressing religiousness quite unrelated?

By beginning with the broadest possible conception of what religious commitment can mean we are trying as much as possible to forestall rejections of our findings based on the belief that we are not really talking about religiousness. Social science research on religion is particularly subject to this kind of dismissal, especially from churchmen, and all dialogue is impossible so long as there is no initial agreement on a common language. Thus we shall try to begin with agreement at least on subject matter. Of course, we maintain no illusion that we can satisfy everyone. Clearly, for those who hold religiousness to be a purely metaphysical phenomenon, beyond the senses and not connected with what men think, or say, or do, our work will be totally irrelevant—mere materialistic concern with mundane appearances.

We are quite content to acknowledge that there may be a metaphysical element in religion which defies scientific scrutiny. But religion as we know it exists in the material world and cannot be comprehended wholly or even primarily in metaphysical terms.

If we examine the religions of the world, it is evident that the details of religious expression are extremely varied; different religions expect quite different things of their adherents. Catholics and many Protestants, for example, are expected to participate regularly in the Christian sacrament of Holy Communion. To Moslems, such a practice is alien. By the same token, the Moslem imperative to undertake a pilgrimage to Mecca during one's lifetime is alien to Christians. Similarly, Hindus are enjoined from eating beef, while Moslems and Jews reject pork, evangelical Protestants abstain from alcohol, and, until recently, Catholics did not eat meat on Friday. These seem to be substantial variations, but we suggest that they are variations in detail. Beyond the differences in specific beliefs and practices, there seems to be considerable consensus among all religions on the general ways in which religiousness ought to be manifested. We propose that these general ways provide a set of core dimensions of religiousness.

Five such dimensions can be distinguished; within one or another of them all of the many and diverse religious prescriptions of the different religions of the world can be classified. We shall call these dimensions: *belief, practice, knowledge, experience,* and *consequences.*[3]

1. The *belief* dimension comprises expectations that the religious person will hold a certain theological outlook, that he will acknowledge the truth of the tenets of the religion. Every religion maintains some set of beliefs which adherents are expected to ratify. However, the content and scope of beliefs will vary not only between religions, but often within the same religious tradition. Within Christianity, the religion with which our present study is concerned, we shall have occasion later to distinguish

---

[3] Some readers will recognize that we have dropped the more abstract names used to designate these dimensions in earlier work. The original names caused both confusion and needless argument (for example, the belief dimension was earlier called the ideological dimension) and we have dropped them here in the interests of clarity.

among various types of beliefs. However, for now we are interested merely to indicate that belief is a dimension of religion, not to establish ways to measure it.

2. Religious *practice* includes acts of worship and devotion, the things people *do* to carry out their religious commitment. Religious practices fall into two important classes:

Ritual refers to the set of rites, formal religious acts, and sacred practices which all religions expect their adherents to perform. In Christianity some of these formal ritual expectations are attendance at worship services, taking communion, baptism, weddings, and the like.

Devotion is somewhat akin to, but importantly different from ritual. While the ritual aspect of commitment is highly formalized and typically public, all known religions also value personal acts of worship and contemplation which are relatively spontaneous, informal, and typically private. Devotionalism among Christians is manifested through private prayer, Bible reading, and perhaps even by impromptu hymn singing.

3. The *experience* dimension takes into account the fact that all religions have certain expectations, however imprecisely they may be stated, that the properly religious person will at some time or other achieve a direct, subjective knowledge of ultimate reality; that he will achieve some sense of contact, however fleeting, with a supernatural agency. As we have written elsewhere, this dimension is concerned with religious experiences, those feelings, perceptions, and sensations which are experienced by an actor or defined by a religious group (or a society) as involving some communication, however slight, with a divine essence, that is, with God, with ultimate reality, with transcendental authority.[4] To be sure, there are marked contrasts in the varieties of such experiences which are deemed proper by different religious traditions and institutions, and religions also vary in the degree to which they encourage *any* type of religious encounter. Nevertheless, every religion places at least minimal value on some variety of subjective religious experience as a sign of individual religiousness.

[4] Glock and Stark, *op. cit.*, chs. 3 and 8.

4. The *knowledge* dimension refers to the expectation that religious persons will possess some minimum of information about the basic tenets of their faith and its rites, scriptures, and traditions. The knowledge and belief dimensions are clearly related since knowledge of a belief is a necessary precondition for its acceptance. However, belief need not follow from knowledge, nor does all religious knowledge bear on belief. Furthermore, a man may hold a belief without really understanding it, that is, belief can exist on the basis of very little knowledge.

5. The *consequences* dimension of religious commitment differs from the other four. It identifies the effects of religious belief, practice, experience, and knowledge in persons' day-to-day lives. The notion of "works," in the theological sense, is connoted here. Although religions prescribe much of how their adherents ought to think and act in everyday life, it is not entirely clear the extent to which religious consequences are *a part* of religious commitment or simply *follow from it*. In any event, we shall not take up the study of religious consequences in this volume. Rather, the whole of Volume Three will be devoted to investigating the social and psychological consequences of commitment.

For our present purposes, we will assume that the initial four dimensions provide a complete frame of reference for assessing religious commitment. But while it is possible to postulate these four aspects of religiousness on analytic grounds, relations among them cannot be explored without empirical data. It is scarcely plausible that they will be entirely unrelated. However, it is equally clear that being religious on one dimension does not necessarily imply being religious on another. An exploration of the connections of these dimensions of religious commitment will be taken up in Chapter 9. However, a few preliminary remarks need to be made here about the relative importance of the various dimensions. Religions may require them all but not value them equally.

For all religions it can be said that theology, or religious belief, is at the heart of faith. It is only within some set of beliefs about the ultimate nature of reality, of the nature and intentions of the supernatural, that other aspects of religion become coherent.

Ritual and devotional activities such as communion or prayer are incomprehensible unless they occur within a framework of belief which postulates that there is some being or force to worship. Similarly, it is plausible to call a rather ignorant believer religious, but not the knowledgeable skeptic. Or, the believer who has not undergone a religious experience could still be called religious, but a person who has religious experiences, but no religious beliefs, is likely to be called psychotic. Indeed, the believer who backslides when it comes to living up to his faith in everyday affairs, may still be defined as religious, but not so the ethical atheist. Thus, the belief dimension can be considered a particularly necessary, but often not sufficient, aspect of religious commitment.

In Christianity, it can be argued, religious practice is the second most valued aspect of religious commitment, not of such primary importance as is belief, but more cherished than the other three. However, in more mystical religions, and some extreme Protestant sects, more importance is placed on religious experience than upon practice.

It should also be noted that there is likely a certain incompatibility between the knowledge and experience dimensions. Religious bodies which place great importance on one seem inclined to give less importance to the other, although both dimensions are given some value in all religions. Modern Christianity seems to give less stress to religious experiences and more to religious knowledge.

While it seems true that these four aspects of religious commitment are not equally valued by religious institutions, all are valued to a considerable extent. Thus, any comprehensive effort to understand religious commitment, must consider each of them. In so doing it will be possible to construct extensive empirical descriptions of patterns of religious commitment, both among American Christians in general, and as comparisons among the major denominations.

Before concluding this chapter, something must be said about a well-known schema for classifying persons according to their religious commitment, and why we have chosen not to incorporate it into this study. This is Gordon W. Allport's important distinction between two types of religiousness, the "intrinsic" and the "extrinsic." [5] Allport's typology is presently enjoying a considerable vogue especially among psychologists. The basis of Allport's distinction is not merely the extent of a person's religious behavior (in the sense we have outlined it in this chapter), but the *motives* for his behavior, and to some extent the *consequences* of his religious behavior for other aspects of his life.

Allport characterizes the extrinsic type of religiousness as:

> utilitarian, self-serving, conferring safety, status, comfort and talismanic favors upon the believer. . . . People who are religious in this sense make use of God . . . [they are] dependent and basically infantile.[6]

The intrinsic type, he describes as follows:

> This kind of religion can steer one's existence without enslaving him to his limited concepts and egocentric needs. One may call this type of religion "interiorized" or "intrinsic" or "outward-centered." In any case, it is the polar opposite of the utilitarian, self-centered, extrinsic view.[7]

Allport's types crosscut the kinds of criteria of religious commitment we have developed earlier in this chapter. Although in order to be religious in Allport's terms all persons must meet our criteria, he seeks to further exclude persons from being "really" or "authentically" faithful on the basis of their instrumental motives for piety or their lack of theological sophistication. While it is interesting that the mainstream of the Christian tradition has given major encouragement to the very sources of belief that Allport discredits,[8] these are, to be sure, most important distinctions. It seems both certain and important that folkish concep-

[5] Gordon Allport, *Religion in the Developing Personality*, Academy of Religion and Mental Health (New York University Press, 1960).

[6] *Ibid.*, p. 33.   [7] *Ibid.*

[8] The New Testament directly appeals to the deprived and promises them comfort. Similarly, conservative Christianity today shows no such "choosiness," but explicitly seeks conversions on the basis of the personal good that follows from faith. Apparently this whole tradition, including hundreds of hymns such as "What a friend we have in Jesus, all our sins and griefs to bear," falls on the "inauthentic" side of the intrinsic, extrinsic distinction.

tions of faith will produce different interpretations of the world (e.g., of political values) than will sophisticated theologies. Similarly, it is very probably the case that people who adhere to faith out of need for psychic security will act upon their faith differently from persons whose commitment is based on high moral purpose. Indeed, these expectations provide a major theoretical basis for Volumes Two and Three of this study.

But for all their importance it seems wise to exclude Allport's distinctions from our definition of religious commitment, for to include in the definition both the motives for commitment and the consequences which follow from it makes it impossible really to ask anything further about commitment. The purpose of all science, including social science, is explanation. But explanation is impossible unless there is something to explain. That is, it must be at least logically possible for assertions to be falsified; elements that are presumed to be related must logically be capable of independent variation. When a relationship between two concepts or elements in a theory is defined as true, independent variation is not even logically possible. For example, if by definition *only* intrinsic religious motives can produce authentic religious commitment, it is impossible to discover what kinds of motives most typically produce religious behavior, or even whether extrinsic motives can on occasion lead to authentic commitment. The reason for this is obvious, intrinsic religious motives and authentic religious commitment have been defined as equivalent. Similarly, if by definition *only* altruistic attitudes *can* follow from religious beliefs (otherwise the belief is inauthentic, extrinsic religion) then it is not possible to see whether the religious training, beliefs, and activities promoted by religious institutions typically do produce admirable results.[9]

Thus, to include Allport's distinctions in the definition of reli-

---

[9] It is recognized that Allport did not initially postulate these relationships as true by definition, but that he constructed his types through intensive psychological study of individual religiousness. However, the finished types present this "true-by-definition" problem for anyone who seeks to employ them in their own research. While Allport's analysis may have provided justification for the types as generalizations—elements may be *related* in the manner which the types suggest—it is hard to estimate the extent to which

gious commitment precludes the possibility of investigating the very questions to which this study is devoted: the part played by religious behavior in contemporary life. While Allport has summarized very important factors relating to religious commitment, they should not be asserted by definition but made subject to investigation as factors influencing or stemming from religious commitment.

An important subsidiary reason for considering Allport's types in some detail is the extent to which they have been improperly employed by religionists as an apologetical and polemical device to dismiss all research findings which question the perfection of the church in the world. Since nearly all social science writing on religion presently must endure attacks based on this device it seems worth a bit of attention here.

Whenever the results of a social science investigation indicate that religious commitment is positively associated with some variety of human failing or folly, a number of religious spokesmen can be counted on to dismiss them by redefining religiousness in a way that excludes all unpleasantness. For example, when an earlier book by the authors reported that persons who hold certain traditional Christian beliefs are very much more likely to be anti-Semitic than are persons who reject such beliefs,[10] many religious spokesmen responded that *only* tolerant attitudes towards Jews are found in *truly* religious persons. Thus, they conclude that the churches bear no moral responsibility for prejudice since pious persons free of anti-Semitism are the *only* intrinsically religious persons, while those who are anti-Semitic are merely extrinsic, inauthentic believers. It must be emphasized that not all

---

he found deviant cases, that is, cases where the relations did not hold. If the correlations were not virtually perfect, then while the data undoubtedly justified his types as generalizations, to adopt them a priori in our study would rule out the possibility of treating the elements of the types as variables. The possibility is open, at this point, for types along similar lines to emerge at the conclusion of our study to sum up our findings. But this is a way of describing findings, not of beginning analysis.

[10] Charles Y. Glock and Rodney Stark, *Christian Beliefs and Anti-Semitism* (New York and London: Harper and Row, 1966).

church spokesmen have taken this position. Most accepted the results as presenting the churches with a challenge to teach their members more adequately the real meaning of the faith. However, some of the most vocal spokesmen did attempt to define the whole problem out of existence.

In taking such a stance, religious spokesmen seem oblivious to the fact that they are thus reading out of the church as inauthentic a major proportion of their most active, loyal, and otherwise most pious members. No such exclusiveness is employed when churches compute the number of their members, or when they accept financial contributions. Furthermore, this is poor theology. The main thrust of Christian theology is that the church is the people of God, and consequently that the church is made up entirely of sinners. Theologically, one is guilty of most sinful pride to think that any selecting criteria could reveal a core group of true Christians, untainted by sin, who constitute the real church.

In the final analysis, of course, theology is beside the point. We are engaged here in sociological matters, with the churches as human institutions embedded in human society, and with assessing the impact of religion for good and evil in the lives of its human membership.

Chapter 2

RELIGIOUS BELIEF[1]

*He that believeth not
shall be damned.
Mark 16:16 (A.V.)*

Virtually everyone agrees that the central feature of Christian commitment is belief. But contemporary theologians disagree considerably over what it is that Christians ought to believe. As a result it is nearly impossible to select any universally acceptable standards either to distinguish the believer from the nonbeliever or to reflect degrees and kinds of convictions among those who profess faith.

In order partly to accommodate different conceptions, we shall develop several independent measures of religious belief. From among these, however, we shall focus primarily on a measure of belief based on acceptance or rejection of the historic doctrines of Christianity. Specifically, we shall define a believer as a person who acknowledges a supernatural realm and who conceives of the supernatural in historic Christian terms—a personal God, a divine Saviour, and a life beyond death.

To insist on these supernatural conceptions as an essential component of our primary assessment of Christian belief will seem both obvious and necessary to many readers. But many others, especially liberal theologians and churchmen, will object to such criteria of belief. They are not agreed upon an alternative statement of what they would call authentic Christian belief, but they reject supernaturalism, at least as we have defined it, as either necessary or central to being a Christian. In fact, some theologians claim that it is principally traditional orthodoxy that today

[1] Portions of this chapter have previously appeared in Charles Y. Glock and Rodney Stark, *Christian Beliefs and Anti-Semitism* (New York and London: Harper and Row, 1966), chs. 1 and 2; and in Charles Y. Glock and Rodney Stark, *Religion and Society in Tension* (Chicago: Rand McNally, 1965), ch. 5.

prevents men from achieving an authentic understanding of Christian truth. This may be superior theology, but it strikes us as inferior sociology. Because of the importance of this problem we shall briefly review our reasons for reaching this conclusion. The reader may remain unconvinced, but it is hoped that some basic considerations will be clarified.

From the very beginning of our inquiry we were aware that we would invite considerable criticism by placing primary reliance on a traditional definition of religious belief; but we felt compelled to do so for two reasons.

One reason is based on the fact that we are primarily interested in accounting for variations in human behavior. In pursuing this quest we are convinced that the difference between holding or not holding supernatural convictions is a very crucial variable. Persons who believe in the supernatural seem very likely to define and respond to the world quite differently from persons who reject supernaturalism. Historically, we suspect that the primary way in which religion has affected human behavior is by inculcating and supporting elaborate conceptions of the supernatural. To blur this distinction by defining religious belief in a way that would ignore supernaturalism, would, in our judgment, preclude study of what may be the most interesting and fruitful aspect of religious belief for the purposes of social science. The question of whether traditional Christian supernaturalism is theologically valid is not germane to sociology. Rather, the question is whether or not these beliefs which are widely associated with Christianity have social and psychological consequences, and if so, what are they? Because we are sociologists, sociological criteria must guide us.

But in addition to this, early in our research it became evident that there is also empirical justification for giving primary attention to supernaturalism in identifying religious belief. In preparing our questionnaire we conducted a number of exploratory interviews with laymen to see how they in fact conceived of their religious convictions. Almost universally we found that the man in the pew defines religious belief in traditional terms. He either accepts the traditional, supernatural tenets of Christianity or locates himself theologically in terms of the extent to which he rejects these beliefs. By and large, laymen are simply unaware of the complicated redefinitions of modern theology. But even those who are aware assess these redefinitions on the basis of the extent to which they omit traditional articles of faith. The contemporary church member who says he is a liberal quite unselfconsciously defines his beliefs by reference to their distance from traditionalism. Historic orthodoxy is the anchor point of his system of reference and he describes his own views in terms of what, from this orthodoxy, he no longer accepts. Since the objects of our study are laymen, not clergymen, we felt this characteristic of lay theology justified a classification based on traditional orthodoxy.

These arguments notwithstanding, there will be some who will continue to discount the centrality of supernaturalism for assessing religious belief among contemporary Christians. Ultimately, of course, the test of our decision is not its theological suitability, but its fruitfulness in accounting for other forms of behavior. As we proceed in the study we shall continue to review this decision. Furthermore, we will develop some alternative criteria of belief in order to make a comparison among criteria possible.

But before making any attempt to measure religious belief, it seems prudent to determine what it is that people who identify themselves as Christians do believe these days. The present chapter is devoted to this descriptive task. The portrait of contemporary belief which follows seems of considerable intrinsic interest because so little is known about the actual religious views of modern Americans; but this portrait will also serve two additional functions. First of all, it will provide a basis for constructing systematic criteria of belief, which we will take up in Chapter 3. Secondly, these descriptive materials will provide some initial insights on two current religious issues: *ecumenism* and *secularization*.

Ecumenism identifies the hopes for a reunification of Christianity. These hopes have been greatly encouraged by a series of recent denominational mergers and by the stimulus to interfaith dialogue provided by Vatican II. In part, the ecumenical dream rests on the assumption that Christians are reaching a common theological outlook, that the old differences have lost much of their force. In this view contemporary denominationalism is an organizational rather than theological affair.

A second widely-discussed aspect of contemporary Christianity is the assumption that traditional theology is being overwhelmed by the secular culture and that American belief is rapidly shifting from a literalistic old-time faith to demythologized modernism. Many younger theologians not only agree that such changes have taken place, but celebrate them as a modern reformation that will soon revitalize the faith.

The question is, of course, have such changes been going on? So far there has been virtually no hard evidence one way or the other and we have had to rely on impressions, fragments of fact, and speculation.

The data in this chapter begin to provide the needed evidence. In assessing the state of current religious belief we shall also construct theological profiles of the various denominations in order to see the extent to which they have adopted similar religious views. Later chapters will furnish other important facts. In the last chapter of this volume we shall attempt a general assessment of the future course of ecumenism and secularization.

With these eventual aims in mind, we may now turn to an examination of the anatomy of contemporary Christian belief.

SUPERNATURALISM

The most universal and basic element in Christian theologies is an elaborate set of assertions about the nature and will of an all-powerful and sentient God. All Christian moral norms and religious practices are justified and understood as deriving from the intent of this Creator of human history. Thus, examining what Americans believe about God and the divine realm seems a fruitful starting point for a more general inquiry into religious belief. Subsequently we shall turn to beliefs in various aspects, intentions of, and obligations to, the divine.

Commentators on the current American scene are virtually unanimous in thinking all but a mere handful of Americans believe in God. Findings from national polls support this assumption; repeated Gallup surveys have found that 96 to 97 percent of all American adults respond "yes" when asked, "Do you, personally, believe in God?" Although a few observers have been somewhat uncomfortable about the seeming lack of sophistication of such an either-or probe, and have wondered how many different images of God were subsumed within this gross summary, most have been content to accept these findings as a ratification of the unchanging character of our religious faith, especially when contrasted with the much lower levels of belief in God disclosed by similar polling in European nations.

Given this virtual unanimity among the general public, it might seem pointless to examine belief in God among *members* of Christian churches.[2] What could possibly be found but universal acceptance? Yet, it seems possible that there might be significant differences in the *images* of God held by different persons as well as in the degree they are certain about their belief. Looking at the data shown in Table 2, it is strikingly apparent that even in a sample of only church members, there are indeed important contrasts both in conceptions of God and in conviction. Furthermore, these variations sharply distinguish the denominations from one another.

In selecting the statement about God that came closest to their own views, only 41 percent of the Congregationalists indicated unquestioning faith in a personal divinity. This proportion rises to 60 percent of the Methodists, 63 percent of the Episcopalians, reaches about the three-quarter mark among the denominations in the center of the table, and is virtually the unanimous response of Southern Baptists and members of the fundamentalist sects. Overall, 71 percent of the Protestants endorsed this traditionally

[2] It will be recalled from the introduction that our examination of religious commitment will be based on two sets of data: the California church-member sample and the national sample of the adult population. We shall follow the practice, where data from both samples are relevant to our inquiry, to present results from church members first and then the results from the national sample.

orthodox position as compared with 81 percent of the Roman Catholics.

Looking at the second line of the table, we may see that the greatest proportion of persons who rejected the first statement did not do so because they held a different image of God, but because they differed in their certainty. While they conceived of a personal divinity, they admitted having doubts about his existence. Denominational differences here too are marked: from 34 percent of the Congregationalists to 1 percent of the Southern Baptists.

The third possible response, line three in the table, is simply a more "doubtful" version of the second and did not draw much support. However, the fourth response category is especially interesting, for it marks a different conception of God, rather than differences in the certainty of faith. Again, contrasts are striking: 16 percent of the Congregationalists, 11 percent of the Methodists, 12 percent of the Episcopalians, down to none of the Southern Baptists thought not of a personal God, but simply of some kind of "higher power." Overall, 7 percent of the Protestants held this deist conception of God, while 3 percent of the Roman Catholics did so.

To complete the findings, it should be noted that 2 percent of the Congregationalists, Episcopalians, and Methodists took an agnostic position (line 5), and 1 percent of the Congregationalists candidly said they did not believe in God.

Looking at the overall figures, if responses to the first four categories are added together, the totals would indicate that 98 percent of both Protestants and Roman Catholics believe to some extent in what they think of God, which is a very close match for the usual Gallup results. What the data reveal, however, is how much variation in the strength of belief and the kind of God believed in is suppressed by a simplistic inquiry.

It must be remembered, however, that the data shown in Table 2 are based on a sample made up entirely of Christian church members in four counties along the western coast of San Francisco. What reason is there to expect that these data bear any resemblance to conditions elsewhere in the nation and in the

Table 2

BELIEF IN GOD (Church-Member Sample)

"Which of the following statements comes closest to what you believe about God?"

	Congregational	Methodist	Episcopalian	Disciples of Christ	Presbyterian	American Lutheran[c]	American Baptist	Missouri Lutheran	Southern Baptist	Sects[d]	TOTAL Protestant	Roman Catholic
Number:[b]	(151)	(415)	(416)	(50)	(495)	(208)	(141)	(116)	(79)	(255)	(2,326)	(545)
I know God really exists and I have no doubts about it.	41%	60%	63%	76%	75%	73%	78%	81%	99%	96%	71%	81%
While I have doubts, I feel that I do believe in God.	34	22	19	20	16	19	18	17	1	2	17	13
I find myself believing in God some of the time, but not at other times.	4	4	2	0	1	2	0	0	0	0	2	1
I don't believe in a personal God, but I do believe in a higher power of some kind.	16	11	12	0	7	6	2	1	0	1	7	3
I don't know whether there is a God and I don't believe there is any way to find out.	2	2	2	0	1	*	0	1	0	0	1	1

I don't believe in God. 1 * * 0 * 0 * 0 0 0 * 0

No answer	2	*	1	4	*	*	2	0	1	0	1	1
Total [a]	100%	99%	99%	100%	100%	100%	100%	100%	100%	100%	99%	100%

* Less than half of 1%.

[a] Some columns fail to sum to 100% due to rounding error.

[b] The number of respondents shown for each denomination in this table is the same for all other tables in this chapter.

[c] American Lutherans are a combination of members of The Lutheran Church in America and the American Lutheran Church. Members of these two denominations were sufficiently alike in their responses to warrant considering them together rather than independently.

[d] Included are The Assemblies of God, The Church of God, The Church of Christ, The Church of the Nazarene, The Foursquare Gospel Church, and one independent tabernacle.

Table 3
BELIEF IN GOD (National Sample)

	"I know God really exists and I have no doubts about it"	
	Number	(percentage)
Unitarian...............................	(9)	22 [e]
Congregational [a]........................	(44)	63
United Presbyterian......................	(75)	67
Protestant Episcopal.....................	(56)	72
Methodist...............................	(217)	78
Presbyterian Church U.S.................	(40)	70
Disciples of Christ [b]......................	(42)	73
American Lutheran bodies [c]...............	(146)	70
Lutheran, Missouri Synod.................	(45)	70
Evangelical and Reformed [a]...............	(28)	71
American Baptist.........................	(91)	82
Southern Baptist.........................	(187)	93
Other Baptist bodies.....................	(90)	86
Sects [d]	(128)	90
Total Protestant..........................	(1,197)	79
Roman Catholic..........................	(507)	85

[a] The Congregational and the Evangelical and Reformed denominations merged several years ago to form a single body under the name of the United Church of Christ. However, because of the extreme contrasts in religious outlook between members of the two original bodies we have presented them here separately under their old names.

[b] Officially The Christian Church.

[c] Included here are the Lutheran Church in America and the American Lutheran Church. There were no important empirical differences between members of these two bodies.

[d] Included in the category of sect were: Assemblies of God, Church of Christ, Church of God, Foursquare Gospel, Free Methodist, Mennonite, Nazarene, Pentecostal, Salvation Army, Seventh Day Adventist, Campbellite, Jehovah's Witnesses, Christian Missionary Alliance, Mission Covenant, and various tiny holiness bodies. Excluded were such groups as Christian Science, Unity, Divine Science, Theosophy, Spiritualists, and other such bodies which most properly should be classified as cults, for our analysis, but since only 11 persons in the sample claimed affiliation with bodies of this type, such a general category seemed futile. Also excluded were persons who claimed affiliation with the various Eastern Orthodox churches, Mormons, and one member of each of the major Asian faiths.

[e] Too few cases for a stable percentage. Presented for descriptive interest only.

population at large? It can immediately be seen in Table 3, however, that these findings are not to be dismissed as "California Christianity." In these data based on a national sample of the adult population, differences in the proportions who "know God really exists and have no doubt about it" range from 22 percent of the Unitarians, 63 percent of the Congregationalists, and up to 93 percent of the Southern Baptists. Overall, roughly three-fourths of the Protestants and 85 percent of the Roman Catholics indicated undoubted faith in God.[3]

The national data generally confirm[4] the findings in the

[3] Two hundred and seventy-two respondents are omitted from denominational tables, namely persons who gave their religious affiliation as Jews, Mormons, None, one of the Eastern or Asian faiths, or various small cults.

[4] Recalling responses to this same question as reported in Table 2 it will be noted that the proportions giving this response are somewhat higher in the national data, especially in the most liberal bodies. There are several reasons for this contrast. The California data were collected by an anonymous questionnaire, while the national data are the product of personal interviews. It seems reasonable to expect that on a matter so heavily sanctioned by social norms as belief in God, having to state one's belief to a stranger (most often a middle-aged, middle-class housewife) would introduce a bias in favor of the most "proper" answer.

As we shall see later, aside from the highly sensitive question of belief in God, on all other belief comparisons the general population is less likely than California church members, to claim firm belief. All California respondents presently resided in a large urban area. Many persons in the national sample lived in rural areas. This rural/urban factor is largely responsible for other differences between the national and the California data: For example, the Methodists appeared to be somewhat less traditional in their religious ideology than the Episcopalians in the California data, although the differences were quite small. However, in the national data they appear to be slightly more traditional than the Episcopalians. The reason for this shift is that the rural/urban effect is of greater significance among Methodists than among Episcopalians. That is, Episcopalians are more predominantly urbanites than are Methodists and therefore when rurals are included in the sample the Episcopalian profile is less affected. Methodists in rural areas make up a greater proportion of the total Methodist membership and consequently cause a greater change between an urban and a national profile. City Methodists are very liberal. Country Methodists are rather conservative.

An additional difference between the national and California data must also be noted: more denominations are represented in the national data. This

church-member sample, that firm belief in God is far from unanimous among Americans, and that the denominations differ importantly in the degree to which their members hold traditional faith
in God.

Gallup studies also report that Americans are virtually unanimous in believing Jesus Christ to be the Divine Son of God. But
in light of our findings about belief in God, we can expect this
faith too needs to be qualified by degree of certainty as well as
differences in the images of Christ.

Table 4 shows that even among church members there are
important contrasts in belief in the divinity of this central figure
of Christianity. The pattern of denominational differences across
the first line of the table is virtually identical to the pattern of
belief in God. Differences range from 40 percent of the Congregationalists who have no doubts that "Jesus is the Divine Son of
God," to 99 percent of the Southern Baptists. The total Protestant figure is 69 percent in contrast to 86 percent among Roman
Catholics.

Variations in the degree to which Christian church members
ratify faith in an orthodox conception of Christ come into even
sharper focus when we examine some specific details of Christol-
ogy. As shown in Table 5, only 57 percent of all Protestants
responded "completely true" when asked to evaluate the statement, "Jesus was born of a virgin," while 81 percent of the
Roman Catholics did so. But even more startling differences can
be observed among the Protestant bodies: from 21 percent of the
Congregationalists, the proportion rises to 99 percent of the
Southern Baptists.

The dispersion among Protestants is even slightly increased
when we examine the second item in the table which reports the
proportions who thought it "completely true" that "Jesus walked
on water." Firm believers in this miracle, commonly credited to

---

is a function of regional differences, and broadens the scope of the study.
Furthermore, many persons in the national sample are not members of any
church congregation, although nearly all claim some denominational tie.
Thus, in the national data findings apply to the churched and the unchurched
alike.

Table 4

BELIEF IN THE DIVINITY OF JESUS (Church-Member Sample)

"Which of the following statements comes closest to what you believe about Jesus?"

	Congregational	Methodist	Episcopalian	Disciples of Christ	Presbyterian	American Lutheran	American Baptist	Missouri Lutheran	Southern Baptist	Sects	TOTAL Protestant	Roman Catholic
Number:	(151)	(415)	(416)	(50)	(495)	(208)	(141)	(116)	(79)	(255)	(2,326)	(545)
Jesus is the Divine Son of God and I have no doubts about it.	40%	54%	59%	74%	72%	74%	76%	93%	99%	97%	69%	86%
While I have some doubts, I feel basically that Jesus is Divine.	28	22	25	14	19	18	16	5	0	2	17	8
I feel that Jesus was a great man and very holy, but I don't feel Him to be the Son of God any more than all of us are children of God.	19	14	8	6	5	5	4	0	0	*	7	3
I think Jesus was only a man, although an extraordinary one.	9	6	5	2	2	3	2	1	1	*	4	1
Frankly, I'm not entirely sure there was such a person as Jesus.	1	1	1	0	1	*	0	0	0	0	1	0
Other and no answer.	3	3	2	4	1	0	2	1	0	1	2	2

* Less than half of 1%.

Table 5

ADDITIONAL BELIEFS ABOUT JESUS (Church-Member Sample)

	Congregational	Methodist	Episcopalian	Disciples of Christ	Presbyterian	American Lutheran	American Baptist	Missouri Lutheran	Southern Baptist	Sects	TOTAL Protestant	Roman Catholic
Number:	(151)	(415)	(416)	(50)	(495)	(208)	(141)	(116)	(79)	(255)	(2,326)	(545)
Jesus was born of a virgin.												
Percentage who said "completely true."	21	34	39	62	57	66	69	92	99	96	57	81
Jesus walked on water.												
Percentage who said "completely true."	19	26	30	62	51	58	62	83	99	94	50	71
Do you believe Jesus will actually return to the earth some day? Percentage who answered:												
Definitely.	13	21	24	36	43	54	57	75	94	89	44	47
Probably.	8	12	13	10	11	12	11	8	4	2	10	10
Possibly.	28	25	29	26	23	18	17	6	0	1	20	16
Probably not.	23	22	17	12	12	6	6	4	1	2	13	11
Definitely not.	25	17	11	6	8	7	5	1	1	3	10	12
No answer.	3	3	6	10	3	3	4	6	0	3	4	4

Christ, form a small minority in the large, liberal denominations, constitute half of Protestants in general, make up 71 percent of the Roman Catholics, and 99 percent of the Southern Baptists.

Like the existence of God, the Saviourhood of Christ produces mixed reactions among Christians. Vast differences also exist among Protestants in the proportions who accept the promise of the "Second Coming," while differences between Protestants in general and Roman Catholics are trivial. Forty-eight percent of the Congregationalists felt Christ will "definitely" or "probably" *not* return to earth as compared with 2 percent of the Southern Baptists. Correspondingly, only 13 percent of the Congregationalists, and 21 percent of the Methodists thought Jesus will "definitely" return as compared with 75 percent of the Missouri Synod Lutherans and 94 percent of the Southern Baptists. Overall, less than half of both the Protestants and Roman Catholics thought the Second Coming was definite, and less than 60 percent even thought such an event probable. Clearly Protestants cannot join together in affirming that old evangelistic phrase, "Christ Crucified, Risen, Coming Again." Indeed, such certainty is held by only a minority of Christian church members.

The extreme contrasts among the various denominations we have seen thus far are matched by widely different views on the authenticity of biblical accounts of miracles. In Table 6 the proportions responding that they believe the "miracles actually happened just as the Bible says they did," vary from 28 percent of the Congregationalists and 37 percent of the Methodists, 69 percent of the American Lutheran bodies, 89 percent of the Missouri Lutherans, to 92 percent of the Southern Baptists. Seventy-four percent of the Roman Catholics ratified miracles in contrast to 57 percent of all Protestants.

Two more central Christian tenets will complete our exploration of American religious beliefs about the supernatural: belief in life after death and belief in the existence of the Devil.

Again we see the marked differences in the proportions holding these beliefs across denominations from left to right in Table 7. While only 36 percent of the Congregationalists are certain there is a life beyond death, 97 percent of the Southern Baptists con-

Table 6

MIRACLES (Church-Member Sample)

"The Bible tells of miracles, some credited to Christ and some to other prophets and apostles. Generally speaking, which of the following statements comes closest to what you believe about Biblical miracles?"

	Congre-gational	Metho-dist	Episco-palian	Disciples of Christ	Presby-terian	American Lutheran	American Baptist	Missouri Lutheran	Southern Baptist	Sects	TOTAL Protestant	Roman Catholic
Number:	(151)	(415)	(416)	(50)	(495)	(208)	(141)	(116)	(79)	(255)	(2,326)	(545)
Percentage who answered:												
"Miracles actually happened just as the Bible says they did."	28	37	41	62	58	69	62	89	92	92	57	74
"Miracles happened but can be explained by natural causes."	32	31	22	16	20	14	16	4	0	3	19	9
Percentage who doubt or do not accept miracles.	32	24	27	14	14	13	9	5	3	5	17	9

Table 7

LIFE BEYOND DEATH (Church-Member Sample)

	Congregational	Methodist	Episcopalian	Disciples of Christ	Presbyterian	American Lutheran	American Baptist	Missouri Lutheran	Southern Baptist	Sects	TOTAL Protestant	Roman Catholic
Number:	(151)	(415)	(416)	(50)	(495)	(208)	(141)	(116)	(79)	(255)	(2,326)	(545)
"There is a life beyond death." Percentage who answered:												
Completely true.	36	49	53	64	69	70	72	84	97	94	65	75
Probably true.	40	35	31	32	21	23	19	10	3	4	24	16
Probably not or definitely not true.	21	13	13	0	7	5	7	4	0	2	9	5
"The Devil actually exists." Percentage who answered:												
Completely true.	6	13	17	18	31	49	49	77	92	90	38	66
Probably true.	13	15	16	34	17	20	17	9	5	5	15	14
Probably not or definitely not true.	78	66	60	38	48	26	29	10	1	5	43	14

sider this a certainty. Greater variation occurs among Protestants on the existence of the Devil, with the proportions who are certain the Devil exists ranging from only six percent of the Congregationalists and 13 percent of the Methodists up to 92 percent of the Southern Baptists. Overall, 38 percent of the Protestants and 66 percent of the Roman Catholics felt certain about the Devil's existence.

These two beliefs were also asked of the national sample of American adults, which contains both church members and the unchurched.

The effect of having the unchurched in the national sample clearly shows up in Table 8. On the existence of the Devil belief is *lower* in nearly all denominations than was reported in Table 7, and in the others it is about equally absent. This clearly suggests

Table 8

THE DEVIL AND LIFE BEYOND DEATH (National Sample)

	Number	Percentage absolutely sure there is a devil	Percentage absolutely sure there is a life beyond death
Unitarian...................	(9)	0	0
Congregational..............	(44)	7	26
United Presbyterian..........	(75)	20	36
Protestant Episcopal.........	(56)	21	35
Methodist..................	(217)	33	42
Presbyterian Church U.S....	(40)	35	43
The Christian Church.........	(42)	29	42
American Lutheran bodies.....	(146)	31	52
Lutheran, Missouri Synod.....	(45)	44	50
Evangelical Reform..........	(28)	39	50
American Baptist............	(91)	47	41
Southern Baptist............	(187)	55	65
Other Baptist bodies.........	(90)	55	59
Sects.....................	(128)	61	67
Total Protestant.............(1,197)		40	50
Roman Catholic.............	(507)	36	48

that persons who actually belong to a congregation are much more likely to have retained their faith in the Devil than are persons who claim the same denomination without belonging to a congregation. Unfortunately, through an accident in preparing the final interview schedule this likely explanation cannot be tested. The question that would have asked respondents in the national sample if they belonged to a specific congregation was inadvertently left out.

The same order of differences between our samples of church members and the general public can be seen on belief in life after death. In all denominations the national data indicate a smaller proportion believe in life after death than was found in the California church-member data.

Perhaps a more important feature of Table 8 is the confirmation of our findings that the religious bodies in America differ greatly in their commitment to traditional theological tenets. Great differences can be seen by reading down the table in the proportions of these denominations who believe in the Devil and in a life beyond death. Americans nationwide are somewhat less likely to be committed to an orthodox religious ideology than are church members in Northern California. Only half of American Protestants as well as Roman Catholics are certain there is a life beyond death, and only four out of ten unreservedly believe in the Devil.

ORIGINAL SIN

Turning to the concept of original sin, a new pattern of denominational schism is revealed in Table 9. At different points on the left-right (liberal to conservative) spectrum, those denominations in a liturgical, or "High Church," tradition are readily distinguishable by their acceptance of original sin. That is, churches that have traditionally emphasized the importance of formal ritual, such as Communion, Absolution, and the like, and which have given greater liturgical emphasis to original sin (which is not amenable to personal efforts to redeem, but can only be absolved through the church), show up at all points of the left-

Table 9
ORIGINAL SIN (Church-Member Sample)

	Congregational	Methodist	Episcopalian	Disciples of Christ	Presbyterian	American Lutheran	American Baptist	Missouri Lutheran	Southern Baptist	Sects	TOTAL Protestant	Roman Catholic
Number:	(151)	(415)	(416)	(50)	(495)	(208)	(141)	(116)	(79)	(255)	(2,326)	(545)
"A child is born into the world already guilty of sin."												
Percentage who answered:												
Completely true.	2	7	⑱	6	21	㊽	23	㊅	43	47	26	㊽
Probably true.	2	4	7	2	7	12	9	4	3	3	6	10
Probably not or definitely not true.	94	87	71	90	68	37	65	9	55	46	65	19

right continuum. Among the very liberal bodies, the Episcopalians stand out from the other less liturgical denominations, 18
percent saying "completely true" as compared with 7 percent of
the Methodists and 6 percent of the Disciples of Christ. In the
center of the table, the American Lutherans, traditionally liturgical, stand out sharply from the less ritualistic Presbyterians and
American Baptists. On the far right, the Missouri Lutherans differ
considerably from the Southern Baptists and the various sects.
Overall, the generally more liturgical Roman Catholics contrast
greatly with the Protestants, 68 percent versus 26 percent. (The
more liturgical denominations have been circled in the table for
easy comparison.)

It is clear that there is a general relationship between belief in
original sin and theological conservatism underlying these data,
so that Lutherans are much more likely to hold this view than the
Episcopalians, yet the marks of the formal doctrine show up all
across the table. The majority of Episcopalians seemingly have
relinquished much of their orthodoxy, but those who retain it tend
to differ from those who have retained orthodox Methodism on
the question of original sin. Thus, on the left of the table the
vestiges of old doctrinal differences on original sin may still be
detected, while on the right these differences retain much of their
traditional force. As we turn to further comparisons of the denominations we shall discover other examples of these differences
between the more and less liturgical bodies.

REQUIREMENTS FOR SALVATION

So far we have examined denominational variations on belief in
some of the central figures and concepts of Christianity. We shall
now turn our attention to Christianity's central concern and
promise: salvation. The questions about salvation are separated
into two general classes: first those beliefs, ritual observances and
works which might be judged necessary requirements for salvation; second those improper beliefs, ritual violations and acts
which might be considered as resulting in certain forfeiture of the
possibility of salvation.

Faith

While Christians have long battled over the question of whether faith *and* works were required to be saved, there has been virtual unanimity that faith was absolutely required. The central tenet of this required faith is belief in Jesus Christ as the Divine Son of God who died to redeem men from their sins. While some Christian traditions hold that more than faith in Christ is required for salvation, all have agreed that there is no salvation outside of Christ.

However, since we have seen earlier that members of American denominations are far from unanimous in crediting Jesus with divinity, it is hardly surprising to find them markedly disagreeing over whether belief in Christ is absolutely necessary for salvation.

Turning to the data in Table 10, we see that holding faith in Christ as "absolutely necessary" is the point of view of a minority among the more liberal denominations. Among the most conservative groups, however, there is virtual consensus about the necessity of faith in Christ for salvation. Overall, 65 percent of the Protestants and 51 percent of the Roman Catholics gave this answer. Recalling the findings on belief in life after death, it seems likely that among all Protestant groups, persons who accept the promise of an eternal salvation beyond the grave are also likely to feel that this eternal reward is contingent upon belief in Christ as Saviour. However, since denominations differ widely in the degree to which they still accept this literal interpretation of New Testament promises, they also differ widely in the degree to which they see faith in Christ as a means to such salvation.

Looking at the second item in Table 10, we see that all denominational groups are less likely to feel that one must hold "the Bible to be God's truth" in order to be saved. Overall, the pattern follows the now familiar increases from left to right, with one notable exception. Though the Southern Baptists have been most unanimous in their assertion of traditional Christian positions, we may see here that they are not importantly different from the center denominations as seeing Bible literalism required for salvation. As we will see in further data, this probably reflects the

Table 10

REQUIREMENTS FOR SALVATION—FAITH (Church-Member Sample)

	Congre-gational	Metho-dist	Episco-palian	Disciples of Christ	Presby-terian	American Lutheran	American Baptist	Missouri Lutheran	Southern Baptist	Sects	TOTAL Protestant	Roman Catholic
Number:	(151)	(415)	(416)	(50)	(495)	(208)	(141)	(116)	(79)	(255)	(2,326)	(545)
"Belief in Jesus Christ as Saviour."												
Percentage who said absolutely necessary.	38	45	47	78	66	77	78	97	97	96	65	51
"Holding the Bible to be God's truth."												
Percentage who said absolutely necessary.	23	39	32	58	52	64	58	80	61	89	52	38

great emphasis placed on faith in Christ by Southern Baptists, and, consequently, they seem less inclined to see other aspects of Christian teaching as crucial for attaining grace.

Ritual Acts

On the basis of our earlier findings concerning original sin, we may anticipate the denominations with ritualistic orientations will stand out from the rest in giving importance to ritual acts as requirements of salvation. This expectation is convincingly borne out by the data in Table 11. Looking at the first item in the table, "Holy Baptism," we see the Episcopalians are markedly different from the neighboring Congregationalists and Methodists; in the center of the table the American Lutherans stand out in sharp relief from the Presbyterians and the American Baptists, and on the right, the Missouri Lutherans differ enormously from the Southern Baptists and the sects. Overall, the generally less ritualistic Protestants differ greatly from the Roman Catholics (35% to 65%). A similar pattern can be observed in the proportions who believed that "regular participation in Christian sacraments, for example, Holy Communion," is "absolutely necessary" to gain salvation. However, fewer persons in all denominations saw this ritual requirement as crucial than did so on baptism. Ritualistic orientations can also be detected on the proportions who thought membership in a Christian church was necessary to salvation, although this view was held by only a small minority of members of any group.

The fourth item in the table not only examines requirements for salvation, but seeks to assess the remnants of the denominational chauvinism and parochialism which once typified Christian schisms. The data clearly indicate that, whether through a pluralistic experience or a general loss of fervor, the days when bitter Christian factions saw themselves as having a monopoly on religious authenticity and legitimacy have passed. While Roman Catholics are still frequently accused of believing theirs to be the single possible road to salvation, only about a quarter (28%) felt that it was "absolutely necessary" to be a member of their particular faith in order to be saved. While they are still more prone to

Table 11
REQUIREMENTS FOR SALVATION—RITUAL ACTS (Church-Member Sample)

	Congre-gational	Metho-dist	Episco-palian	Disciples of Christ	Presby-terian	American Lutheran	American Baptist	Missouri Lutheran	Southern Baptist	Sects	TOTAL Protestant	Roman Catholic
Number:	(151)	(415)	(416)	(50)	(495)	(208)	(141)	(116)	(79)	(255)	(2,326)	(545)
"Holy Baptism" Percentage who said absolutely necessary.	11	19	39	32	28	58	25	78	19	46	35	65
"Regular participation in Christian sacraments, for example, Holy Communion." Percentage who said absolutely necessary.	7	10	27	22	17	36	15	55	10	31	22	39
"Membership in a Christian Church." Percentage who said absolutely necessary.	7	8	17	22	13	21	13	33	14	24	16	23
"Being a member of your particular religious faith." Percentage who said absolutely necessary.	3	6	7	8	8	14	12	16	16	25	11	28
"Prayer." Percentage who said absolutely necessary.	39	48	44	62	52	67	55	67	57	87	55	54

this view than Protestants, only 11 percent of whom took this position, the overwhelming majority of Catholics rejected the belief that only Catholics could be saved. Among Protestants, the proportions giving this response increased among the Lutherans, the Baptists, and the sect members but here too, only a small minority agreed.

Turning to more personal ritual requirements for salvation, we may see that Christians generally feel that prayer is absolutely necessary for redemption. Again looking at the left-hand side of the table, we may note that among the Congregationalists, Methodists, and Episcopalians, fewer than half view prayer as absolutely necessary. This probably reflects their lower concern for, and acceptance of, the promise of salvation in general. The denominations in the center of the table show a majority are concerned with prayer. However, proportions do not increase as we move to the more conservative groups except for the sects. Again, this probably reflects the great emphasis that the conservatives place on faith in Christ.

Works

Having become accustomed, in previous tables, to seeing increases from left to right in the proportions holding any act of faith or ritual as necessary for salvation, it may come as something of a surprise to see these trends reverse in Table 12. Nevertheless, examining the first item in the table, "Doing good for others," it is obvious that (except for the sects) a much higher proportion of persons in the denominations on the left than in those on the right consider this absolutely necessary for salvation.[5] Whether or not members of the more conservative groups basically admire "good deeds," they are not inclined to give them any special relevance for salvation. These findings are even more striking when we consider that the absolute proportions of persons in churches on the left who think doing good for others is

[5] As will be discussed in Chapter 3, sect members tended to respond to this battery of items unselectively. That is, while most persons rated some items as more important than others, sect members tended to rate all as important.

Table 12

REQUIREMENTS FOR SALVATION—WORKS (Church-Member Sample)

	Congregational	Methodist	Episcopalian	Disciples of Christ	Presbyterian	American Lutheran	American Baptist	Missouri Lutheran	Southern Baptist	Sects	TOTAL Protestant	Roman Catholic
Number:	(151)	(415)	(416)	(50)	(495)	(208)	(141)	(116)	(79)	(255)	(2,326)	(545)
"Doing good for others." Percentage who said absolutely necessary.	58	57	54	64	48	47	45	38	29	61	52	57
"Loving thy neighbor." Percentage who said absolutely necessary.	59	57	60	76	55	51	52	51	41	74	58	65
"Tithing." Percentage who said absolutely necessary.	6	7	9	12	10	13	16	7	18	48	14	10

required for salvation is higher than the proportions of members of these same groups thinking faith in Christ is absolutely necessary. Indeed, *fewer* persons in the liberal churches were certain of the existence of life beyond death than thought doing good was absolutely necessary for salvation. To explain this seemingly inconsistent behavior, we may suggest that these responses on "doing good" by persons who essentially rejected the traditional notion of salvation, represent their desire to ratify the ethical components of their religious outlook regardless of the context of their response. Indeed, given their lack of commitment to orthodox theology, ethics are likely the central component of their religious perspective.

This relatively larger support for good works among churches on the left is duplicated on the second item in the table, "Loving thy neighbor." However, the decline in proportions saying absolutely necessary is only moderate from left to right, and in general one might say that American denominations pretty much agree on this issue.

Turning from these two more personal forms of works to the more formal and institutionally oriented matter of tithing, it is clear that Christians in general are not inclined to connect this act with salvation. Only 14 percent of the Protestants and 10 percent of the Roman Catholics thought tithing absolutely necessary for salvation. Among the Protestant groups the proportions giving this response increase slightly from the left groups to those on the right. But only among members of the sects does any sizeable portion take this position.

In summary, these data have shown marked contrasts among Christian denominations in their conceptions of what is required for salvation.

BARRIERS TO SALVATION

Improper Faith

We have seen that Christians in general place great emphasis on faith in Christ as essential for salvation, although the denominations differ greatly on this question. We shall now attempt to assess the degree to which this position is translated into judgments about the kinds of religious faith which would automatically preclude the possibility of salvation. Looking at the data in Table 13, the same patterns among denominations found on requiring faith in Jesus for salvation are to be seen in rejecting the possibility of salvation for non-Christians. However, the extension of the positive requirement to the negative sanction is far from complete. Many in all denominations who held faith in Christ as absolutely necessary for salvation were unwilling correspondingly to deny the possibility that persons outside the Christian faith could be saved. For example, only 14 percent of the Protestants and 4 percent of the Roman Catholics said that "being completely ignorant of Jesus, as might be the case for people living in other countries," would definitely prevent salvation. Among Protestants, the proportions taking this position varied from a mere handful of Congregationalists, Methodists, Episcopalians, and Disciples of Christ to 36 percent of the Missouri Lutherans, and 41 percent of the Southern Baptists. However, an additional and sizeable group of Christians were somewhat inclined to accept this view. Twenty-five percent of the Protestants and 24 percent of the Roman Catholics thought ignorance of Jesus would "possibly prevent" salvation. Again, differences among Protestants varied greatly from the left denominations to the fundamentalist groups on the right.

Moving to the next item, 10 percent of the Protestants and 1 percent of the Roman Catholics thought it impossible for a Jew to be saved. Again, there were great contrasts among Protestant groups. One percent of the Congregationalists and 3 percent of the Methodists and Episcopalians took this position, while 31 percent of the Missouri Lutherans and 25 percent of the Southern Baptists saw no hope for Jews to be saved. Again, a sizeable group thought it "possible" that a Jew could not be saved, and taken together, more than half of the members of the groups at least doubted the possibility of a Jew's gaining salvation. These proportions increased when the question of salvation for a Hindu was raised. Forty percent of the Missouri Lutherans and 32 percent of the Southern Baptists felt that followers of the Hindu

Table 13
BARRIERS TO SALVATION—IMPROPER FAITH (Church-Member Sample)

	Congregational	Methodist	Episcopalian	Disciples of Christ	Presbyterian	American Lutheran	American Baptist	Missouri Lutheran	Southern Baptist	Sects	TOTAL Protestant	Roman Catholic
Number:	(151)	(415)	(416)	(50)	(495)	(208)	(141)	(116)	(79)	(255)	(2,326)	(545)
"Being completely ignorant of Jesus as might be the case for people living in other countries."												
Percentage who said it would definitely prevent.	3	7	3	8	11	15	17	36	41	32	14	4
Percentage who said it would possibly prevent.	13	23	16	38	24	29	31	28	39	46	25	24
"Being of the Jewish religion."												
Percentage who said it would definitely prevent.	1	3	3	8	7	16	7	31	25	23	10	1
Percentage who said it would possibly prevent.	6	9	10	18	12	16	25	23	28	33	15	11
"Being of the Hindu religion."												
Percentage who said it would definitely prevent.	1	5	4	10	14	20	14	40	32	37	15	2
Percentage who said it would possibly prevent.	12	11	12	28	15	22	25	16	27	31	17	13

faith would definitely be prevented from gaining salvation, and 15 percent of Protestants overall took this position as compared with 2 percent of Roman Catholics.

In summary, a substantial minority of American Christians consider persons in non-Christian religions as beyond the hope of salvation.

Violations of Proper Ritual

The data in Table 14 show that American Christians attach little relevance for salvation to violations of the sabbath and "taking the name of the Lord in vain." Though we might expect conservatives to attach most importance to keeping the sabbath, and indeed they do, surprisingly 19 percent of the Roman Catholics also see this as definitely preventing salvation. All Christian groups are more likely to think cursing could definitely prevent salvation than they were to invest sabbath violation with such consequences. As might be expected, the more conservative groups were slightly more inclined to connect cursing with obstacles to salvation. However, Missouri Synod Lutherans differed sharply from all other groups on this question, and 41 percent thought salvation would be denied to those taking the name of the Lord in vain. Roughly a quarter of both the Protestants and Catholics shared in this judgment.

Improper Acts

Drinking is no longer regarded as a certain road to damnation by American Christians. Only 8 percent of Protestants and 2 percent of Roman Catholics said drinking would definitely prevent salvation. Only among the Baptists and the followers of fundamentalist sects did more than a handful attach temperance to their scheme of salvation, as seen in Table 15.

Virtually no Protestants (only 2%) thought the practice of artificial birth control would prevent salvation, but perhaps even more interesting and surprising, *less than a quarter of the Catholics held this view*. Whether or not Catholics approve of birth control, more than three-quarters of them are unwilling to agree it carries the supreme penalty of damnation.

Table 14
BARRIERS TO SALVATION—VIOLATIONS OF PROPER RITUAL (Church-Member Sample)

	Congregational	Methodist	Episcopalian	Disciples of Christ	Presbyterian	American Lutheran	American Baptist	Missouri Lutheran	Southern Baptist	Sects	TOTAL Protestant	Roman Catholic
Number:	(151)	(415)	(416)	(50)	(495)	(208)	(141)	(116)	(79)	(255)	(2,326)	(545)
"Breaking the Sabbath."												
Percentage who said it would definitely prevent.	2	4	5	4	6	5	4	5	15	26	8	19
"Taking the name of the Lord in vain."												
Percentage who said it would definitely prevent.	13	19	17	26	20	26	21	41	27	64	26	28

Table 15

BARRIERS TO SALVATION—IMPROPER ACTS (Church-Member Sample)

	Congregational	Methodist	Episcopalian	Disciples of Christ	Presbyterian	American Lutheran	American Baptist	Missouri Lutheran	Southern Baptist	Sects	TOTAL Protestant	Roman Catholic
Number:	(151)	(415)	(416)	(50)	(495)	(208)	(141)	(116)	(79)	(255)	(2,326)	(545)
"Drinking liquor." Percentage who said it would definitely prevent.	2	4	2	0	2	2	9	1	15	35	8	2
"Practicing artificial birth control." Percentage who said it would definitely prevent.	0	0	2	2	1	3	1	2	5	4	2	23
"Discriminating against other races." Percentage who said it would definitely prevent.	27	25	27	34	22	20	17	22	16	29	25	24
"Being anti-Semitic." Percentage who said it would definitely prevent.	23	23	26	30	20	15	13	22	10	26	21	20

The last two items in the table seem especially interesting and repeat the denominational pattern seen in evaluation of good works as relevant to salvation. On virtually all other items exploring possible barriers to salvation, the conservative bodies have shown the greatest propensity to see them as preventing salvation. However, on questions of racial discrimination and anti-Semitism, the conservatives (except the sects) are the *least* likely of all religious groups to see them as relevant to salvation. Thus, while 27 percent of the Southern Baptists thought cursing would definitely prevent salvation, only 10 percent of them viewed anti-Semites as disqualified from entrance into God's Kingdom, and only 16 percent saw racial discrimination as a definite barrier. On the other hand, while only 13 percent of the Congregationalists thought that taking the name of the Lord in vain would definitely prevent salvation, 27 percent gave this response on racial discrimination and 23 percent on anti-Semitism. Perhaps an even more suggestive contrast appears when we consider that about half of the members of all denominations thought it absolutely necessary to "Love thy neighbor" in order to be saved.

To sum up this section on salvation, we have seen that Christian denominations differ greatly in their beliefs about what a man must do in order to be saved. While most denominations give primary importance to faith, the liberal Protestant groups are inclined to favor good works. Protestant groups in a ritualistic tradition and the Roman Catholics place greater emphasis on the sacraments and other ritual acts than do those from low church traditions.

THE "NEW DENOMINATIONALISM"

These data on the theological outlook of the various Christian churches reveal much about the nature of contemporary denominationalism. It has come to be commonly believed both by churchmen and social scientists in America that contemporary Christianity was coming to a theological consensus, that the historic diversities upon which Christianity splintered has corroded leading to a convergence of religious perspectives. It has become fashionable to speak of the "common religion" of Americans and to believe that denominationalism is now based upon organizational rather than theological considerations. But the findings in this chapter suggest that such a view is superficial. While old differences may have passed away—differences over adult versus infant baptism, and the like—new ones have appeared virtually unnoticed. As we shall consider in detail in Chapter 11, these new cleavages occur over the basics of traditional Christian faith. The radical theological reformulations of the twentieth century have not been confined to the leading seminaries or to scholarly tomes. Among the rank and file of the mainline Protestant denominations they also receive widespread support. Clearly secularization has importantly gone on in these denominations. Admittedly these laymen do not cast their religious perspective in the semantic complexities of the professional theologians, but theirs is an equally demythologized faith. On the other hand one observes denominations like the Southern Baptists where the rank and file seem almost unanimously committed to the traditional faith of their fathers. Thus, perhaps at no prior historical moment have the Christian denominations been so divided on basic tenets. These divisions, it must be emphasized, are not between Christians and secular society (although this is certainly true as well), but exist substantially *within* the formal boundaries of the Christian churches.

This theological fragmentation of Protestantism also has important implications for research. The data in this chapter seriously challenge the common social science practice of comparing Protestants and Roman Catholics. While Protestant-Catholic contrasts are often large enough to be notable, although often, too, remarkably small, they seem inconsequential compared to differences found *among* the Protestant groups. Indeed, the data indicate that the overall impression of American Protestantism produced when members of all denominations are treated as a single group (the Total Protestant column in the tables) at best bears resemblance to only a few actual denominations making up the Protestant collectivity. Indeed, in some instances these "average Protestants" do not closely correspond to any *actual* denomination.

This suggests that to a great extent when we speak of "Protestants," as we so often do in the social sciences, we spin statistical fiction. Thus, it seems unjustified to consider Protestantism as a unified religious point of view in the same sense as Roman Catholicism. Not that Roman Catholicism is monolithic either; clearly there are several theological strands interwoven in the Catholic church too but there is at least some justification for treating them collectively since they constitute an actual, organized body. Protestantism, on the other hand, includes many separately constituted groups and the only possible grounds for treating them collectively would be if they shared in a common religious vision. Since this is clearly not the case, we shall have to change our ways.

This change in the way we should conceive of Protestantism seems to offer considerably more interesting prospects. It ought to be much more significant to discover what Protestant groups Catholics are similar to and different from on particular issues than to focus on the crude comparisons between the average Protestant and the average Roman Catholic which is characteristically what past studies have done. Furthermore, the data we have presented in this chapter illustrate the importance of examining differences *among* Protestant bodies, for denominationalism seems still to be a major fact in American religious life.

In the concluding chapter we shall again consider the new character of denominationalism and the impact of secularization in American life. But now our interest turns to using these data to devise means for classifying persons according to the degree their religious commitment is manifested through belief.

Chapter 3

MEASURING RELIGIOUS BELIEF

*Thou art weighed in the balances
and art found wanting.*
Daniel 5:27 (A.V.)

We have seen that among contemporary Christians there is great variation in religious belief. In this chapter we shall seek means to characterize this variation—to classify persons systematically according to the degree to which their religious commitment is reflected in belief. Such classification is necessary if we are to examine subsequently the relationship between belief and other aspects of religious commitment: practice, experience, and knowledge. It is also necessary for the work to be reported in Volumes Two and Three where we shall investigate the social and psychological sources and consequences of belief.

The tasks of this chapter would be much easier if we could rely on a single measure of religious belief which would provide a simple ordering of respondents along a continuum from belief to unbelief. But even though we are committed to measuring belief primarily on the basis of traditional supernaturalism, it is not self-evident that it may be treated as a unitary phenomenon. Furthermore, we mean to give some consideration to beliefs that are not explicitly supernatural.

The different versions of belief necessary to provide an adequate basis for study appear to be these:

Foremost among aspects of belief is the extent to which the traditional supernatural doctrines are acknowledged. We shall order people along a continuum from those who unequivocally affirm the traditional Christian teachings about the divine to those who reject them outright. The measure thus created will be called the Orthodoxy Index.

A second aspect of belief is what we have called *particularism*.

It also presupposes supernaturalism, but in addition postulates that only one version of the nature of the supernatural is true. In traditional Christianity, particularism is manifested in the doctrine that only through Christ is it possible to be saved, and that all who believe otherwise are necessarily damned. Thus, particularism interprets orthodoxy in absolute terms as the exclusive religious truth.

A third manifestation of faith suggested by the descriptive data in the last chapter is based on commitment to doctrines of Christian ethics, those teachings about how men ought to act towards their fellows in the spirit of the Sermon on the Mount. It is an empirical question whether belief of this type is distinct from, or merely a component of, orthodoxy. On impressionistic grounds it seems reasonable to expect that persons might retain a commitment to Christian ethics while rejecting all supernaturalism. Consequently, it seemed wise to explore ethicalism as a possible independent cluster of religious beliefs. In so doing we can also perhaps accommodate those Christians who object to supernaturalism as a criterion of belief.

Finally, we shall examine the extent to which Christian theology functions as a source of ultimate meaning—provides a systematic solution to questions about the meaning and purpose of life. It seems to be one of the marks of emerging modern man that he rejects not only specific systems of ultimate meaning, but also the possibility of *any* definitive system of answers to such questions. In the last part of this chapter we shall see whether this trend is present in the contemporary churches.

We may now take up each of these means for measuring religious belief in greater detail.

ORTHODOXY

From the belief items we examined in Chapter 2, four were selected from which to construct the Orthodoxy Index. These are: the existence of a personal God, the divinity of Jesus Christ, the authenticity of biblical miracles, and the existence of the Devil.

In constructing the index, a respondent received a score of one for *each* of these belief questions on which he expressed his certainty of the truth of the orthodox Christian position. Respondents received a score of zero for each item on which they acknowledged doubt or disbelief about the orthodox response.[1] Thus, a person could score as high as four, by being certain in his faith on all four items, or as low as zero by reporting doubt or disbelief on all four.

As can be seen in Table 16, the Orthodoxy Index shows the same relationship to various denominations that was observed in our examination of the items included in it. Furthermore, among both Protestants and Catholics, although less so among the latter, the Orthodoxy Index distributes respondents widely, revealing many degrees of ideological commitment.

Having constructed the index, it remains to be demonstrated whether it sensitively measures what we mean it to. Looking at the first three items in Table 17, we see that among both Protestants and Catholics the index powerfully and consistently predicts acceptance of other central Christian tenets: life beyond death, the virgin birth, and Christ's walking on water.

But the bottom two items in the table give even more impressive demonstrations of the sensitivity and validity of the index. Here it is used to predict tenets which are central to *some* traditions in Christianity, *but not to others*. The concept of original sin, is advocated by some Protestant theologies and eschewed by others, and the table shows that while the proportions feeling this concept is absolutely true rise across categories of the index, even among the most orthodox Protestants only about half take this position. However, for Roman Catholics, original sin is proper doctrine, and acceptance of it is predicted powerfully by the Orthodoxy Index. Thus, the index does not predict just *any* Christian teaching, but is sensitive to disagreements among Chris-

---

[1] Two hundred and sixteen persons who failed to answer one or more of the items were not scored. Subsequent analysis revealed them to be proportionately distributed across all categories of orthodoxy and their deletion has no influence on subsequent findings.

Table 16

ORTHODOXY AND DENOMINATION (Church-Member Sample)

Orthodoxy Index	Congre-gational	Metho-dist	Episco-palian	Disciples of Christ	Presby-terian	American Lutheran	American Baptist	Missouri Lutheran	Southern Baptist	Sects	TOTAL Protestant	Roman Catholic
Number:	(141)	(381)	(373)	(44)	(457)	(195)	(130)	(111)	(76)	(247)	(2,155)	(500)
High 4	4%	10%	14%	18%	27%	43%	43%	66%	88%	86%	33%	62%
3	18	20	23	36	29	20	20	21	9	10	21	19
2	18	23	21	23	16	12	18	7	3	3	16	6
1	12	17	18	7	12	12	7	5	0	0	12	4
Low 0	48	30	24	16	16	13	12	1	0	1	18	9
	100%	100%	100%	100%	100%	100%	100%	100%	100%	100%	100%	100%

Table 17

VALIDATION OF THE ORTHODOXY INDEX

		Percentage who answered "Completely true"				
		Orthodoxy Index				
		Low				High
Belief question		0	1	2	3	4
1. "There is a life beyond death."	Protestants	12	35	65	79	97
	Catholics	15	24	47	71	96
2. "Jesus was born of a virgin."	Protestants	6	20	38	74	96
	Catholics	11	10	59	91	98
3. "Jesus walked on water."	Protestants	3	11	24	63	95
	Catholics	9	10	41	66	92
4. "A child is born into the world already guilty of sin."	Protestants	3	8	12	22	55
	Catholics	9	19	47	61	89
5. "The Pope is infallible in matters of faith and morals."	Protestants	2	2	2	2	1
	Catholics	11	19	44	63	85
Number of cases on which percentages are based.	Protestants	394	248	339	454	720
	Catholics	46	21	32	97	304

tian denominations. This is further demonstrated by belief in Papal infallibility, a specifically Roman Catholic teaching. A handful of Protestants in each category of orthodoxy—most of whom probably erred in marking their response—accept this statement as "completely true." However, among Catholics, acceptance is accurately predicted by the Orthodoxy Index. These findings clearly indicate that our index, made up of general belief items, is also a valid register of orthodoxy specific to particular groups. As a result, we can use one index to classify all our respondents rather than having to make separate indices for classifying members of the various denominations.

ORTHODOXY NATIONWIDE

Having constructed an Orthodoxy Index upon the data collected from the sample of California church members it remains to build a similar measure for use in the national sample. In so doing we shall be able to make some generalizations concerning the present state of Christian orthodoxy in American society as a whole.

The three questions on religious belief from the national sample presented in the last chapter—belief in God, in the Devil, and in life after death—were combined in the same way as items in the church-member study to form an Orthodoxy Index. The distribution of scores on this index in the various denominations is shown in Table 18. As in the California data, differences within

Table 18

ORTHODOXY (National Sample)

	Low			High	
	0	1	2	3	
Unitarian (8)	75	25	0	0	100%
Congregational (43)	37	35	23	5	100%
United Presbyterian (74)	27	35	24	14	100%
Protestant Episcopal (53)	21	38	26	15	100%
Methodist (214)	19	32	25	24	100%
Presbyterian Church U.S. (38)	24	26	24	26	100%
The Christian Church (39)	26	28	23	23	100%
American Lutheran bodies (147)	23	27	23	27	100%
Lutheran, Missouri Synod (45)	27	22	13	38	100%
Evangelical Reform (28)	25	25	14	36	100%
American Baptist (91)	16	29	22	33	100%
Southern Baptist (186)	5	20	31	44	100%
Other Baptist bodies (91)	8	29	18	45	100%
Sects (131)	7	17	24	52	100%
Total Protestant (1,187)	18	27	23	32	100%
Roman Catholic (506)	14	32	25	29	100%

Protestantism are very great: none of the Unitarians, 5 percent of the Congregationalists, and 14 percent of the United Presbyterians scored high on the index, that is, affirmed their faith in all three traditional tenets. On the other hand, 44 percent of the Southern Baptists, 45 percent in smaller Baptist bodies, and 52 percent of those belonging to small sects scored high. However, the overall Protestant and Catholic differences seem relatively trivial—32 percent of all Protestants scored high while 29 percent of the Roman Catholics did so.

But perhaps the most important finding in the table is that the overwhelming proportion of Americans today do not adhere to a pristine orthodoxy. Less than a third overall were firmly committed to these three beliefs, and only in the small Protestant sects were as many as half classifiable as highly orthodox. Indeed, 45 percent of America's Protestants and 46 percent of the Roman Catholics fall in the *bottom* two categories of the Orthodoxy Index. Thus it is clear that "Old Time" Christian orthodoxy in all its certainty is not the predominant religious perspective of modern America. Whether Protestant or Catholic, the average American does not firmly ratify this group of traditional doctrines.

These findings raise the issue of secularization. A number of recent commentators have claimed that American religion during the twentieth century has become increasingly secularized; that the mystical and supernatural elements of traditional Christianity have been replaced by an increasingly skeptical and demythologized religious outlook.[2] These data suggest that this has indeed occurred. While it is true that we have no comparable information on the religious beliefs of nineteenth-century Americans, there seem compelling historical grounds for suggesting that the average mid-nineteenth-century American Christian would have scored high on our Orthodoxy Index. If this assumption is warranted then it is clear that substantial changes have in fact taken place.

But these changes have not been universal. While data in this chapter suggest that they have also occurred among church mem-

[2] Charles Y. Glock and Rodney Stark, *Religion and Society in Tension* (Chicago: Rand McNally, 1965), ch. 5.

bers they have not occurred to the same extent in all denominations. If it can be assumed that most Congregationalist and Episcopalian church members of a hundred years ago held a firm belief in God, in the divinity of Jesus, biblical miracles, and the existence of the Devil, it is clear that profound changes have occurred in these bodies. Only a small minority subscribe to all of these beliefs today. But among the most conservative Protestant groups—such as the Southern Baptists, the Missouri Lutherans, and the sects—the erosion has been considerably less. Secularization, then, is more widespread in the general population than it is among church members only, and, further, within the churches it has occurred to a much greater extent in the liberal and moderate bodies than in the conservative groups.

Thus far in this chapter we have constructed measures of orthodoxy to classify both church members and the nation at large. We must now consider a less general feature of Christian theology than orthodoxy.

RELIGIOUS PARTICULARISM

Particularism, our second measure of religious belief, was initially developed in an earlier volume on the Christian sources of anti-Semitism.[3] There, we attempted to show theoretically and empirically that certain kinds of theologies imply a narrow and precisely defined sphere of persons who qualify as properly religious. Such precise and narrow conceptions of proper religious status, tantamount to religious chauvinism, we identified as religious particularism.[4]

Most simply put, religious particularism is the belief that only one's own religion is permissible, that all others are false, foolish, or wicked. In our pluralistic, modern society particularism can take broader or narrower forms. Some may feel that any faith is

[3] Charles Y. Glock and Rodney Stark, *Christian Beliefs and Anti-Semitism* (New York: Harper and Row, 1966), especially ch. 2.

[4] *Webster's New World Dictionary* defines particularism as: "the theological doctrine that redemption is possible only for certain individuals."

acceptable so long as it acknowledges a Supreme Being. Others may limit religious legitimacy to Christians, and still others may reject all but their own specific denomination, or even certain members of their denomination.

Whether broad or narrow, a particularistic outlook discredits all persons whose religious status lies beyond the boundaries of what is seen as the "true" faith. Obviously, the wider these boundaries, the fewer *actual* persons and groups who will be excluded. Thus, the breadth of particularism has great practical importance for those concerned about conflict among men. However, the quality of seeing one's own group as singularly blessed is the same in broader and narrower instances.

An abiding issue in the Christian tradition is the question of salvation, what is required of men in order that they may be saved. This suggests that if one wants to discover particularistic conceptions of religious legitimacy the place to look is at the criteria imposed on salvation: Who are viewed as eligible for entrance to God's Kingdom?

In the preceding chapter we examined a number of questions bearing on the conditions governing salvation. Three of these proved especially suitable to plot the boundaries of an increasingly more specific particularism.

The first question sought to determine whether or not respondents saw salvation as limited to Christians: as shown back in Table 10, more than half of the church members (65% of the Protestants and 51% of the Catholics) thought it "absolutely necessary" for salvation that a person believe in "Jesus Christ as Saviour." Furthermore, a sizeable minority thought this "probably would help in gaining salvation." Clearly, a majority of Christian church members felt that only Christians qualify for salvation.

However, it becomes evident in considering the second item bearing on particularism that many Christians are reluctant to translate this positive requirement into a negative sanction. Far fewer persons in all denominations were willing to say that "being completely ignorant of Jesus, as might be the case for people living in other countries," would "definitely" prevent salvation (see Table 13). A sizeable proportion, however, felt this could "possibly" be the case.

The third item to be treated as a measure of particularism drastically narrows the scope of salvation from Christians in general to the person's own denomination. Here again fewer persons took an adamant position (Table 11), but again a goodly number displayed muted chauvinism by responding that membership in their particular faith "probably would help" gain salvation.

Following the indexing procedures used in the measures of orthodoxy, these three items were scored to provide a summary measure of religious particularism. Further analysis established the validity of the Particularism Index.[5]

Turning to Table 19 we may see the relative extent of particularism in the Christian denominations. Particularism is a rather uncommon religious outlook among Congregationalists (9% scored high) and Methodists (17%). It is more common among American Lutherans and American Baptists, where about a third score high. However, it is the prevailing point of view in such conservative bodies as the Missouri Lutherans (62%), the Southern Baptists (66%) and the various sects (75%). Overall, about a third of both Protestants and Roman Catholics hold this chauvinistic view of their own special religious legitimacy.

PARTICULARISM NATIONWIDE

Two questions were available in the national study from which to construct a measure of religious particularism: that only persons who believe in Jesus Christ may be saved, and identifying Christians (or even one's own denomination) as God's "chosen people" today. Overall, 64 percent of the Protestants nationally thought a person who did not accept Jesus could *not* be saved. Only 29 percent of the Roman Catholics did so.

Similarly, Catholics are less likely than Protestants to think that Christians are presently God's chosen people. While 35 per-

[5] Glock and Stark, *op. cit.*, 1966.

Table 19

RELIGIOUS PARTICULARISM (Church-Member Sample)

	Congre-gational	Metho-dist	Episco-palian	Disciples of Christ	Presby-terian	American Lutheran	American Baptist	Missouri Lutheran	Southern Baptist	Sects	TOTAL Protestant	Roman Catholic
Number:	(132)	(356)	(362)	(45)	(422)	(181)	(116)	(96)	(67)	(215)	(1,992)	(461)
Particularism Index												
High	9%	17%	16%	29%	24%	36%	41%	62%	66%	75%	31%	33%
Medium	48	50	46	64	56	46	47	37	33	25	46	51
Low	43	33	38	7	20	18	12	1	1	0	23	16

cent of the Protestants thought Christians were presently God's chosen people, 21 percent of the Roman Catholics did so.

These two items were combined into a simple Index of Particularism. Persons who both thought only those who believed in Jesus could be saved, and who thought Christians were the current chosen people of God were scored high on the index. Persons who accepted either one of these two notions were scored as medium, and those who rejected both were scored low on the Particularism Index.

Table 20 shows the national distribution of particularism

Table 20
PARTICULARISM (National Sample)

	Low	Medium	High	
Unitarian (8)........................87		13	0	100%
Congregational (43)...................19		58	23	100%
United Presbyterian (74)...............22		49	29	100%
Methodist (214)......................17		42	41	100%
Presbyterian Church U.S. (38)...........10		50	40	100%
The Christian Church (39)..............21		38	41	100%
American Lutheran bodies (147).........17		41	42	100%
Lutheran, Missouri Synod (45)...........13		38	49	100%
Evangelical Reform (28)................18		50	32	100%
American Baptist (91)................. 6		51	43	100%
Southern Baptist (186)................. 5		44	51	100%
Other Baptist bodies (91)..............11		39	50	100%
Sects (131).......................... 7		37	56	100%
Total Protestant (1,187)...............13		44	43	100%
Roman Catholic (506).................24		49	27	100%

among the Christian denominations. While 43 percent of the Protestants accepted both beliefs, only 27 percent of the Roman Catholics took this position. Conversely, only 13 percent of the Protestants rejected both beliefs while 24 percent of the Catholics did so. Particularism is lowest among the Unitarians (0% scored high) followed by the Congregationalists (23% scored high) and highest among the sect members (56% scored high). Overall, the belief that one has a monopoly on religious virtue seems relatively common. This, as we shall see in Volume Three, has profound implications for religious prejudice in modern life.

A comparison between Tables 19 and 20 suggests that the general American public is more given to particularism than are California church members. Part of this is produced by the fact that particularism *is* considerably less widespread in the Far West than in any other region of the country and this seems to affect church members as well as the unchurched. But a major part of this difference between the national and the church-member data is produced by the fact that the indices are not identical. To receive a maximum score on particularism a church member had to think that salvation was restricted to his own denomination. This item was not asked of the national sample. Because this question is considerably more extreme than those used in scoring respondents nationwide, it makes the church members appear less particularistic than the general public. Thus, a descriptive contrast between the two tables is inappropriate.

ETHICALISM: AN ALTERNATIVE TO ORTHODOXY?

It is clear enough from the preceding data that a substantial number of contemporary Christians no longer hold traditional orthodox religious conceptions. But what are the terms in which they do define their religiousness, if any?

Recently it has become clear that for many theologians and religious intellectuals religion means a concern with ethics. If traditional Christianity was primarily preoccupied with the man-to-God relationship, newer theologies, beginning with the Social Gospel Movement in the late nineteenth century, have been shifting primary religious concern to the man-to-man relationship. As Langdon Gilkey has recently put it, the two main themes of traditional Christianity were "purity of doctrinal belief, and the demand for personal holiness (or, more specifically, freedom from vice). . . ." [6] But recently, in Gilkey's judgment, these concerns have been receding rapidly "at least among the more serious and thoughtful Christians—so that love of the neighbor has become . . . the accepted ethical desideratum of full Christian existence." [7]

Supernaturalism, in our judgment, is still the crucial variable in contemporary religious identity, at least in the general population, if not among the intelligentsia. But for all that we must consider the extent to which ethicalism may be a religious phenomenon distinct from orthodoxy. Do those who have rejected orthodoxy exhibit a greater commitment to religious ethics?

Unhappily, we can only explore this question to a limited extent. Questions ideal for independently tapping ethicalism were not included in the questionnaire. However, some partly suitable and suggestive data are available.

An initial clue was provided in the preceding chapter where it was seen that although persons in the more conservative denominations were much more likely than those in liberal groups to attach extensive criteria to salvation, they notably shied away from criteria based on man-to-man rather than man-to-God relationships. Thus, Southern Baptists, for example, were more likely to think swearing would definitely prevent salvation (27%) than to think discriminating against other races would have this effect (16%). Similarly, conservatives put "Holding the Bible to be God's truth" well ahead of "Doing good for others" or "Loving thy neighbor" as necessary for salvation. Conversely, liberals gave less emphasis to man's relation to God, and put correspondingly heavier weight on his relation to his fellows. Indeed, we remarked earlier that more liberals supported ethicalism as necessary for salvation than actually believed in traditional salvation beyond the grave.

These data suggest that the ethical impulse does underlie the religious consciousness of many modern Christians who have rejected orthodox supernaturalism. However, in trying to measure

[6] "Social and Intellectual Sources of Contemporary Protestant Theology in America," *Daedalus* (Winter, 1967), p. 73.

[7] *Ibid.*

this impulse less inferentially we face difficulties. Many liberals, who we would suspect to be among the most ethically concerned, failed to answer these questions on the criteria of salvation because they rejected the whole concept. Similarly others who did answer rejected all criteria of salvation. Thus their possible ethical concerns were not tapped because of the way the questions were asked. This reduces the utility of any measure based on these items. Still if it can be shown that ethicalism and orthodoxy are nonetheless unrelated or even negatively related—despite these manifest biases—the case that ethicalism has become for many a substitute for supernaturalism can be considered strong indeed. That is, the bias in the data will tend to make orthodoxy and ethicalism appear to be more related than they actually are since the least orthodox persons are disproportionately and selectively omitted from this set of measurements.

Two items were selected to construct an Ethicalism Index: the importance placed upon "Doing good for others," and "Loving thy neighbor" for gaining salvation. Persons received two points for each of these they held to be "absolutely necessary"; one point for each they said would "probably help," and no points for any item they rejected as not affecting salvation. Thus the Ethicalism Index ranges from four (holding both to be absolutely necessary to zero (rejecting both).[8]

Table 21 shows the denominational distributions on the Ethicalism Index. Overall, 48 percent of the Protestants and 53 percent of the Roman Catholics felt both of these criteria were absolutely necessary for salvation and scored high on the index (4). Variation within Protestantism is quite extensive, however. The proportion scoring high on ethicalism systematically falls from the more liberal denominations such as the Congregational-

---

[8] Those who did not answer the battery of questions because they reject the concept of salvation were omitted. Respondents who answered the battery but rejected all requirements for salvation are included. These two groups of respondents might very well have revealed ethical concerns had the questions been asked in a different form. Consequently, the Ethicalism Index probably under-represents the number in the sample who reject orthodoxy, but who nevertheless are committed to Christian ethics.

Table 21
ETHICALISM (Church-Member Sample)

	Congregational	Methodist	Episcopalian	Disciples of Christ	Presbyterian	American Lutheran	American Baptist	Missouri Lutheran	Southern Baptist	Sects	TOTAL Protestant	Roman Catholic
Number:	(147)	(387)	(393)	(48)	(474)	(201)	(133)	(111)	(70)	(243)	(2,207)	(516)
Ethicalism Index												
High 4	52%	51%	51%	60%	43%	41%	43%	37%	33%	61%	48%	53%
Medium 2–3	42	45	45	40	46	43	41	41	27	32	42	45
Low 0–1	6	4	4	0	11	16	16	22	40	7	10	2

ists where 52 percent scored high, on down to 33 percent of the Southern Baptists. Indeed, the largest proportion of Southern Baptists scored at the lowest end of the index (40%) while only minute proportions of liberals (4% to 6%) so totally rejected the implications of ethicalism for salvation. The single exception to this liberal-conservative trend is provided by members of the various small Protestant sects. These groups showed the greatest proportion of high scorers on ethicalism (61%). This at first seemed mysterious. On all other data in this chapter sect members have behaved like other conservatives. The answer lay in their unselectivity on the criteria of salvation. A reexamination of sect members' responses to the salvation items reveals that for all practical purposes these people think *everything* bears on salvation. Thus, even on tithing, rejected as bearing on salvation by the overwhelming majority of persons in other conservative bodies, nearly a majority of sect members (48%) thought it "absolutely necessary" for salvation. As a result of seeing salvation as penetrating to almost all matters of behavior and belief, sect members tended simply to agree to all suggestions put by the battery of items. As a result of constructing (through necessity) our measure of ethicalism from the battery of questions asking about criteria for salvation, sect members scored very high as they would have on *any scale* made from items posed in this fashion. (By the same token liberal scores are suppressed because so many had no criteria of salvation having no conception of salvation itself.)

Nonetheless, defective though it may be, this index does lend some support to suggestions that persons who have rejected orthodox supernaturalism predicate their religious identity upon man-to-man ethicalism. Support for "Love of neighbor" and "Doing good for others" is highest in bodies where traditional orthodoxy is weakest.

Table 22 further corroborates this point and also demonstrates the validity of the index despite its imperfections. The items used to build the scale were socially neutral, they only referred to unspecified "neighbors" or "others." Thus, persons who are prejudiced against certain groups such as Negroes or Jews are not

Table 22
VALIDATION OF THE ETHICALISM INDEX

| | Ethicalism Index | | |
	Low	Medium	High
Protestants *	(199)	(859)	(908)
Percentage who believe "being anti-Semitic" would have no influence on salvation.	73	28	15
Percentage who believe "discriminating against other races" would have no influence on salvation.	73	26	13
Percentage high on Orthodoxy Index.	73	50	50
Roman Catholics	(11)	(229)	(276)
Percentage who believe "being anti-Semitic" would have no influence on salvation.	64	22	20
Percentage who believe "discriminating against other races" would have no influence on salvation.	64	20	15
Percentage high on Orthodoxy Index.	73	75	85

* Members of the various Protestant sects have been excluded.

automatically forced to take an anti-ethics position. Rather, persons were allowed to score high for holding ethical attitudes regardless of whether or not they were able to apply them to concrete "others." Nevertheless, it seems instructive that those who accepted these neutral man-to-man principles extend them to reject racial and religious prejudice as well, while those who scored low on the index overwhelmingly believed prejudice also had no bearing on salvation. Thus, only 15 percent of the Protestants who scored high on ethicalism believed that "being anti-Semitic" would have no bearing on salvation, while 73 percent of those scored low on the index felt prejudice against Jews was irrelevant in attaining salvation. Similarly, only 13 percent of those high on ethicalism disregarded "discriminating against other races," while again 73 percent of those scored low did so. Nearly identical patterns can be seen among Roman Catholics. These data provide some grounds for thinking the index is a relatively reliable measure of ethical commitment.

But the main finding in the table is the connection between orthodoxy and ethicalism. Among Protestants, while the most orthodox place vastly more emphasis than do the less orthodox on doctrinal purity and personal holiness for gaining salvation, those scored low on ethicalism are considerably more likely to be orthodox than are those scored high on ethicalism; 73 percent of the least ethical are highly orthodox while 50 percent of the most ethical are highly orthodox. This supports the contention that ethicalism and orthodoxy can be mutually exclusive roots of religious identity. There is a slight tendency for Protestants to be either orthodox and non-ethical, or ethical and unorthodox.

Among Roman Catholics, the relationship is weaker but reversed. Those higher on ethicalism are slightly more likely to be highly orthodox than are those lower on ethicalism. This suggests that the emphasis given by the Catholic church to the social (as opposed to personal) responsibilities of the proper Christian has borne some fruit. For Catholics, adherence to traditional orthodoxy is not entirely at the expense of the traditional ethics of the Sermon on the Mount. In a previous study we found that Roman Catholics were also less likely than Protestants to be prejudiced against Jews and linked these differences to the Catholic emphasis of tolerance and social justice.[9] These data in Table 22 reinforce our earlier judgments. Evangelical Protestantism tends to take a miraculous view of social justice, that if all men are brought to Christ social evils will disappear through divine intervention. Thus they concentrate their energies on conversion and evangelism and largely ignore social issues except for occasional efforts to make unlawful what they judge to be personal vices. They also largely ignore the empirical fact that "born-again" and regenerated Christians remain noticeably sinful and thus offer their followers little guidance in ethical behavior. The Catholic Church,

[9] Glock and Stark, *op. cit.*, 1966.

on the other hand (and increasingly also the liberal Protestant bodies), assumes the sinfulness of man and is concerned to offer moral guidance for the conduct of man-to-man relationships. These tendencies, we suggest, lie beneath our finding that ethicalism is somewhat related to orthodoxy among Catholics, but the two are negatively related among Protestants. In later volumes in this study we shall examine these questions further and also seek the implications of ethicalism for other kinds of behavior.

THEOLOGY AS A SOURCE OF ULTIMATE MEANING

One final matter may be considered in examining religious belief—religion as a source of ultimate meaning. Defining religion in such terms is a recurring theme in contemporary theology, particularly among theologians who reject traditional criteria of religious belief.

We shall explore, in a general way, the degree to which contemporary Christian church members feel that their religious perspective does satisfactorily provide them with a value orientation, a theology that can interpret and give meaning to their existence. Beyond this we shall also inquire how they came by their point of view, if indeed they have one. How many embraced their religious outlook after a period of questioning and seeking truth; how many have simply grown up with their religion? In examining these questions we shall construct a typology of the ultimacy of religious belief, based not upon the theological content of respondent's views, but the degree to which they say their religious ideology functions for them as a system of ultimate meaning.

To investigate these modes of religious commitment, respondents were asked: "How sure are you that you have found the answers to the meaning and purpose of life?" For convenience in explication we shall affix a descriptive label to each of the response categories to this item. The complete item and findings appear in Table 23.

The *Conformists* are those persons who are "quite certain" they know the meaning and purpose of life, and report they "pretty much grew up knowing these things." Such individuals

Table 23

CERTAINTY AND CONCERN ABOUT BELIEF (Church-Member Sample)

"How sure are you that you have found the answers to the meaning and purpose of life?"

	Congre-gational	Metho-dist	Episco-palian	Disciples of Christ	Presby-terian	American Lutheran	American Baptist	Missouri Lutheran	Southern Baptist	Sects	TOTAL Protestant	Roman Catholic
Number:	(151)	(415)	(416)	(50)	(495)	(208)	(141)	(116)	(79)	(255)	(2,326)	(545)
Percentage who answered:												
I am quite certain and I pretty much grew up knowing these things.	23	26	20	30	29	39	34	43	44	49	31	49
I am quite certain although at one time I was pretty uncertain.	16	16	25	22	25	19	28	27	46	36	25	19
Percentage Certain	**39**	**42**	**45**	**52**	**54**	**58**	**62**	**70**	**90**	**85**	**56**	**68**
I am uncertain whether or not I have found them.	36	32	29	32	28	23	24	18	5	5	25	17
I am quite sure I have not found them.	11	8	8	0	5	6	3	3	0	1	5	4
I don't really believe there are answers to these questions.	12	14	14	10	10	10	5	6	4	1	10	8
No answer	2	4	4	6	3	3	6	3	1	8	4	3

seemingly have never had occasion to question seriously the religious perspective they were taught in childhood, and have been content to conform to this early training. The Conformist pattern is markedly related to denomination; about a quarter of the members of more liberal denominations are this type, as compared with more than 40 percent of the Missouri Lutherans and Southern Baptists, up to virtually half of the Roman Catholics (49%). Overall, Conformists make up the slightly most common type among Protestants, 31 percent reporting this pattern.

The *Converted* are "quite certain" they know the answers now, but were once "pretty uncertain." While it is likely these respondents were also raised in a religious tradition, at some time in their lives they seriously doubted, or perhaps even rejected this training. Thus, they have come to their present state of certainty after reflection and doubt, and can be considered converts in the sense of having changed their religious outlook, at least from a previous position of uncertainty. The Converted type is much more common among the conservative and proselytizing groups, such as the Southern Baptists where they constitute the modal type. In all, 25 percent of the Protestants and 19 percent of the Roman Catholics classified themselves as converts.

Adding together these two types, since they share a present certainty about the meaning and purpose of life, striking denominational differences emerge (see the boldface percentages in the table). Thirty-nine percent of the Congregationalists, 42 percent of the Methodists, 62 percent of the American Baptists, and 90 percent of the Southern Baptists consider themselves "certain" about the ultimate interpretation of existence. Thus, the degree to which their religious faith provides a clear solution to questions of ultimate meaning varies greatly among the Protestants.

The *Doubtful* are those who replied they were "uncertain whether or not" they had found the answers. This is the modal type of Congregationalist (36%), Methodist (32%), and Episcopalian (29%) church member, but is much less commonly found among the more conservative groups. Overall, 25 percent of the Protestants and 17 percent of the Roman Catholics doubted the religious perspectives presently available to them. Likely some of these people are incipient converts who will eventually embrace a religious explanation of life. However, they are also probably relatively available for recruitment to other systems of belief. In any event, it seems significant indeed that so large a proportion of actual church members are unconvinced of the validity of Christian perspectives.

The *Disaffected* candidly admit they are "quite sure" they have not found a satisfactory interpretation of ultimate meaning. This is the least common religious stance (5% of all Protestants, and 4% of Roman Catholics), yet a meaningful proportion of those from the more liberal denominations fit this type. These persons too are potentially recruitable to some system of ultimate explanation. It must be made clear that such recruitment need not be to religious outlooks, but could as well be to some humanistic weltanschauung, such as those offered by science, radical politics, or a variety of other philosophical systems.

The *Unavailable* not only do not accept any ultimate solutions to the question of meaning, they reject the existence of such answers. We have used the term Unavailable to indicate that, unlike either the Doubtful or Disaffected types, such persons are not currently available for conversion to any ultimate meaning system, since they discredit the validity of all such existential explanations. This type is found among both Protestants (10%), and Catholics (8%), and is somewhat more common in the liberal than the conservative groups. Although they continue a formal affiliation with a religious body, about one out of ten church members rejects the possibility of explanations for the meaning and purpose of life.

In conclusion, this chapter has selected means for measuring several varieties of religious belief. The most general of these is the Orthodoxy Index, which classifies persons according to the degree to which they personally adhere to the traditional theological tenets of their faith. In addition we have developed the concept of religious particularism, a kind of religious patriotism, and shown the extent to which modern Christians think theirs is the only legitimate faith. Means for classifying persons in terms of their concern for ethicalism were also developed.

Finally, we have seen that the degree to which church members find their theological perspective functions to provide them with solutions to ultimate meaning varies greatly. This, too, is an aspect of belief which we shall consider later in this study.

Chapter 4

RELIGIOUS PRACTICE—RITUAL

Remember the
Sabbath day, to keep it holy.
Exodus 20:8 (A.V.)

Religious practice is defined as the expectation held by all religious institutions that the faithful will observe and perform certain rites and sacred or liturgical acts. In Chapter 1 two varieties of religious practice were distinguished. One kind of religious practice has a formal and public character. The second is relatively informal and typically private. In this chapter we shall examine the formal variety, or what we have called *ritual commitment*. In Chapter 5 we shall take up *devotionalism*, the more informal kind of religious practice.

While the nature of required rituals varies greatly from one religion to another, all known religions impose some such behavioral standards on commitment. Kingsley Davis wrote of religious ritual that it

> is highly circumscribed as to time and place, expressive of internal attitude, symbolic of unseen powers. It can include any kind of behavior known, such as the wearing of special clothing, the recitation of certain formulas, and the immersion in certain rivers; it can include singing, dancing, weeping, bowing, crawling, starving, feasting, reading, etc.[1]

Whatever forms they take, religious rituals are widely regarded by sociologists as playing an extremely important role in the maintenance of religious institutions: Through rituals religions reinforce commitment to their system of beliefs about the nature and intentions of the supernatural. As Davis put it, "Ritual helps to remind the individual of the holy realm, to revivify and strengthen his faith in this realm."[2]

[1] Kingsley Davis, *Human Society* (New York: Macmillan, 1948–49), p. 534.
[2] *Ibid.*

One of the ways ritual has this effect is through the generation of public gatherings. It is largely through rituals that religion constitutes a truly social phenomenon, a gathering of persons for religious reasons to take part in religious activities. Such social circumstances provide the occasions and the means for a collective reaffirmation of the meaning and sacredness of religion, for it is most commonly in such circumstances that people *feel* religious.

In principle the ritual aspects of religion are subordinate to the theological, for rituals can only have meaning as they are warranted by an ideology. However, because ritual activities are typically the most visible, and in a sense most tangible, aspects of religious commitment, in practice they often receive greater emphasis than does ideology. Furthermore, because of this great visibility ritual requirements are subject to more effective control than are theological standards, and similarly the violation of ritual requirements poses a very overt threat to religious authority. A man can easily keep his religious beliefs a secret, but his failure to fulfill his ritual obligations is quickly revealed.

It is quite possible, of course, that ritual obligations will be fulfilled perfunctorily, by merely going through the motions. The fact that a great number of persons in many of the mainline Protestant churches, as seen earlier, reject most of the traditional beliefs of their religion suggests that this may often occur. Later, we shall want to see more exactly how important religious beliefs are for the performance of ritual.

For the present analysis, we shall define ritual commitment to include only religious practices which are performed in the presence of others, whether these may be done in the confines of a church or at home. Attendance at worship services and participation in the sacrament of Holy Communion are the most obvious of these. We shall also include taking part in the organizational life of the church, contributing funds, and saying grace at meals as further manifestations of ritual commitment. Contributions at first glance may seem more a private than a public act. However, since contributions are known to persons other than the contributor, we have elected to classify them under ritual commitment rather than under devotionalism.

We have already reported in Chapter 2 that the majority of modern American Christians do not commonly credit traditional ritual practices as necessary to achieving personal salvation. Just what importance do they place upon them then? How frequently do they perform ritual acts, and what kinds do they perform? And how do members of the various denominations differ in their ritual commitment?

Worship

The most common mode of ritual participation in America is attendance at Sunday worship services. On no other activity do the churches place so great an investment and their efforts to generate a committed membership are commonly gauged by their success in achieving regular attendance at Sunday services. Turning to Table 24 we may see how successful the contemporary churches are in this regard. The data in the table are based entirely on persons who are actually members of specific church congregations, yet the liberal Protestant bodies, on the left of the table, are able to get only a bare majority of their members to attend worship services nearly every week or better. Indeed, *less* than half of the Congregationalists rate their own attendance as weekly or nearly every week (the boldface figures). The proportion of such attenders rises to about two-thirds among the somewhat more conservative churches and on up to 84 percent of the Southern Baptists, and 93 percent of those in the small sects. These denominational differences within Protestantism greatly resemble those found on adherence to orthodox theology which suggests that ritual practice and orthodox belief will be highly interrelated. We shall consider this question in Chapter 9.

For Roman Catholics, regular attendance at Mass is given extreme emphasis in church teachings. Indeed, extended absence from Mass ultimately places a Catholic outside the church. As can be seen in the table, this emphasis on Mass attendance results in a higher proportion of weekly or nearly weekly attenders

Table 24

CHURCH ATTENDANCE (Church-Member Sample)

"How often do you attend Sunday worship services?"

	Congregational	Methodist	Episcopalian	Disciples of Christ	Presbyterian	American Lutheran	American Baptist	Missouri Lutheran	Southern Baptist	Sects	TOTAL Protestant	Roman Catholic
Number:	(151)	(415)	(416)	(50)	(495)	(208)	(141)	(116)	(79)	(255)	(2,326)	(545)
Percentage who answered:												
Every week.	15	23	31	34	29	34	39	43	59	80	36	70
Nearly every week.	30	28	25	34	29	31	36	30	25	13	27	10
Total nearly weekly or better	**45**	**51**	**56**	**68**	**58**	**65**	**75**	**73**	**84**	**93**	**63**	**80**
At least once a month.	33	26	24	18	27	22	17	19	8	4	21	7
At least once a year.	18	16	16	8	13	11	4	7	4	2	11	10
Less than once a year.	1	4	2	4	1	*	1	0	3	0	2	2
Never.	2	1	1	0	*	1	1	0	0	1	1	2

* Less than half of 1%.

among Catholics than among Protestants. Only 63 percent of all Protestants report attending nearly weekly or better while 80 percent of the Roman Catholics do so. Of Protestant bodies, only the Southern Baptists and sect members are better church attenders than are Catholics. These Protestant-Catholic differences are seemingly general. A number of studies of European populations have also revealed this greater regularity of attendance among Catholics.[3]

So far we have been talking about a combined total of those who attend every week and those who attend nearly every week (shown in boldface figures). However, of even greater interest is the contrast between Catholics and Protestants who attend *every* week. Seventy percent of the Catholics say they attend *every* week while only 36 percent of the Protestants do. Thus, Catholics who attend Mass with any regularity overwhelmingly attend with complete regularity, indeed the vast majority of Catholics are "perfect" attenders. By contrast, the vast majority of Protestants fall short of this standard. Only among the Southern Baptists and the sects do more than half attend every week, and only 15 percent of the Congregationalists do so.

Having examined these contrasts in church attendance among church members, we may now study these same differences in the general American population, shown in Table 25. Here similar though not equivalent patterns can be seen. The figures in the first column, "about once a week or more," are comparable to those shown in boldface in Table 24 for "nearly weekly" attendance. In all denominations attendance is considerably lower in the total population than among only church members, as would be expected. Among Americans who identify themselves with one of the Protestant denominations, the churches fall far short of getting a majority to attend church regularly. Relative to the church-member sample, denominational differences are not very great. Protestant-Catholic differences persist, however. As compared to 38 percent of the Protestants, 70 percent of those Americans who call themselves Catholics attend about once a week.

[3] See Charles Y. Glock and Rodney Stark, *Religion and Society in Tension* (Chicago: Rand McNally, 1965), chs. 10, 11.

Table 25

CHURCH ATTENDANCE (National Sample)

	"About how often do you attend worship services?"				
	Once a week or more	Once a month or more	One or 2 times a year	Less than once a year	
Unitarian (9).....................	11	44	33	11	99%
Congregational (44)...............	37	38	16	9	100%
United Presbyterian (76)...........	29	37	21	13	100%
Protestant Episcopal (57)...........	38	34	21	7	100%
Methodist (218)...................	33	32	28	7	100%
Presbyterian Church U.S. (40)........	35	35	18	12	100%
The Christian Church (42)...........	34	21	24	21	100%
American Lutheran bodies...........	34	39	22	5	100%
Lutheran, Missouri Synod (46)........	46	29	17	8	100%
Evangelical and Reformed (28).......	36	43	18	3	100%
American Baptist (92)...............	37	38	17	8	100%
Southern Baptist (187).............	39	44	14	3	100%
Other Baptist bodies (92)..........	38	36	18	8	100%
Sects (132)......................	57	16	17	10	100%
Total Protestant (1,209)............	38	34	20	8	100%
Roman Catholic (507).............	70	16	12	2	100%

Clearly the Catholic Church generates more widespread commitment to participation in worship services. But, as we shall see, Protestants exhibit a greater rate of "success" in generating other forms of ritual participation.

Mass Media Worship

Since the advent of the broadcasting media it is no longer necessary to be physically present to partake of religious worship services. While it is certain that no church has ever suggested that watching services on television or listening to the radio was the moral equivalent of personal attendance, by flooding of the airwaves every Sunday morning the churches may have inadvertently given considerable support to such practices. Indeed, the mass media have produced a new phenomenon in religion—the independent radio preacher who is supported by mail contributions from a regularly listening, but permanently unseen, flock. Even some members of regular congregations have come to prefer this form of worship. As one of our respondents wrote:

> I am an elderly widow and I have been a Baptist all my life, but I don't attend services but once or twice a year now. Because my church broadcasts its Sunday service over the radio I am able to worship regularly in my home. This is much better for me as going to church takes too much out of me, getting a place to park and walked 2–3 blocks, and then in the winter there is the rain. I don't want you gentlemen to think I am just lazy. I get up every Sunday morning and get dressed-up for church just like I always did. This way I show my respect for the Lord and I feel in the same Sunday mood as when I used to go to services. Then I turn on my radio and first I hear another Baptist church service that comes on before our church, and then I hear my own pastor give the message. I find it much more rewarding to go to services in my own home, there are so many folks in church who don't sit still, and who rustle and cough, and even some who sleep! This is very distracting and makes it hard for me to feel the true comfort of the word. . . . Sometimes Mrs. ————— who lives down the block comes here and listens with me and then we have a good dinner afterwards. So I can't mark your question right. I do attend church every Sunday (two services) but I don't go to church much. I also listen to services nearly every evening on radio too.

Thus, for some proportion of Americans, church "attendance" has ceased to be a public activity. It is debatable whether consumption of mass media worship services ought to be discussed here, or placed in the next chapter on devotionalism; but since this item will not be included in our empirical measure of ritual participation, the question is not an urgent one and for sheerly descriptive purposes we have chosen to include it with the ritual items.

Turning to the data in Table 26 we can see that only a small

Table 26

MASS MEDIA WORSHIP (Church-Member Sample)

"Do you ever make a point of listening to or watching religious services on radio or television?"

	Congre-gational	Metho-dist	Episco-palian	Disciples of Christ	Presby-terian	American Lutheran	American Baptist	Missouri Lutheran	Southern Baptist	Sects	TOTAL Protestant	Roman Catholic
Number:	(151)	(415)	(416)	(50)	(495)	(208)	(141)	(116)	(79)	(255)	(2,326)	(545)
Percentage who answered:												
Regularly.	7	7	7	8	10	8	13	13	28	31	12	6
Sometimes.	34	39	37	52	39	48	39	40	44	45	40	38
Very seldom.	30	28	24	28	30	25	30	26	20	18	26	29
Never.	27	25	31	10	19	15	14	21	6	4	20	25
No answer	2	1	2	2	3	3	3	1	1	2	2	2

proportion of Christian church members "regularly" listen to or watch religious services (12% of the Protestants and 6% of the Catholics) but large numbers do so "sometimes" (40% of the Protestants and 38% of the Catholics). Among the Protestant bodies mass media religious participation is most common in the very conservative churches with 28 percent of the Southern Baptists and 31 percent of those in sects doing so regularly. Thus, among Protestants, those bodies among whom regular church attendance is the highest are the same ones among whom media participation is highest. Indeed, further analysis of the data showed that *persons who were the most active church-goers were much more likely to watch or listen regularly to media services than those who were irregular attenders*. This suggests that for most of those people who draw upon mass media religion it is in addition to, rather than in lieu of, active church participation. Furthermore, the vast majority show little consistent interest in mass media services.

Communion

The minimum requirement to remain a Catholic in good standing is to perform the "Easter duty," that is to receive Holy Communion at least once each year. Protestant bodies differ greatly in the emphasis placed on communion. Some of the more liturgical Protestant bodies, such as the Episcopalians and the Lutherans, place considerable importance on communion; others, such as the Methodists and Baptists hold communion services much less frequently and give it little emphasis. All in all, Catholics would be expected to be much more likely than Protestants to have received communion at least once in the preceding year. But this is not the case, as can be seen in Table 27. Eighty percent of all Protestant church members reported they received communion "in the last year," while only 70 percent of the Catholics did so. Only among the Methodists and the Southern Baptists [4] did a smaller proportion report taking communion than did so among

---

[4] A slight terminological confusion may account for the low showing among Southern Baptists who often seem not to recognize that what they call "the Lord's Supper" is commonly called communion.

Table 27

PARTICIPATION IN COMMUNION (Church-Member Sample)

"Have you received Holy Communion in the last year?"

	Congregational	Methodist	Episcopalian	Disciples of Christ	Presbyterian	American Lutheran	American Baptist	Missouri Lutheran	Southern Baptist	Sects	TOTAL Protestant	Roman Catholic
Number:	(151)	(415)	(416)	(50)	(495)	(208)	(141)	(116)	(79)	(255)	(2,326)	(545)
Percentage who answered yes.	79	67	85	92	84	89	86	92	48	80	70	

Catholics. How can this be understood? It seems plausible that for Roman Catholics, religion is much more likely to be an all or nothing affair than it is for Protestants. Protestants tend to be "good" members, while Catholics are either "excellent" or "poor." Recalling Table 24 where church attendance was shown, while Protestants are much less likely than Catholics to attend every week, *they are no more likely than Catholics to attend less than once a month*. Furthermore, precisely the same number of Catholics (70%) reported attending Mass weekly as reported receiving communion in the last year, and the data showed that these were virtually all the same people. Catholics who fall short of the ideal in Mass attendance seemingly rarely take communion, whereas a great host of Protestants who are only moderately frequent church attenders do participate in communion. In achieving participation in the ritual of communion, the Protestant churches are more successful than the Catholic church.

Organizational Participation

The life of the churches is made up of much more than worship services. It includes mission societies, choirs, Bible study groups, ladies organizations, clubs for young couples, and similar activities. In contemporary Christianity particularly among Protestants a great deal of emphasis is placed upon these activities, upon gaining effective member participation in a broad spectrum of church-related groups and enterprises. We shall now assay the success of the churches in achieving such participation.

Table 28 shows how many evenings in an average week respondents said they spend in church or in church-related activities. The majority of church members, 55 percent of the Protestants and 70 percent of the Roman Catholics, typically do not spend *any* evenings in church activities. Thirty percent of the Protestants and 26 percent of the Catholics usually spend one night a week in church and 15 percent of the Protestants and 5 percent of the Catholics spend two or more nights a week in religious activities. Overall, then, Protestants are rather more likely than Catholics to spend their evenings in church activities. However, this participation differs considerably among the Prot-

Table 28

EVENINGS IN CHURCH (Church-Member Sample)

"In an average week, how many evenings do you spend in church, including church meetings such as study groups which may not actually meet in the church building?"

	Congregational	Methodist	Episcopalian	Disciples of Christ	Presbyterian	American Lutheran	American Baptist	Missouri Lutheran	Southern Baptist	Sects	TOTAL Protestant	Roman Catholic
Number:	(151)	(415)	(416)	(50)	(495)	(208)	(141)	(116)	(79)	(255)	(2,326)	(545)
Percentage who answered:												
"Two or more."	4	8	3	12	7	10	17	8	52	67	15	5
"One."	28	33	24	36	30	35	38	38	27	27	30	26
"None."	68	57	73	52	63	55	44	54	21	6	55	70

estant bodies. While 73 percent of the Episcopalians spend no evenings in church, only 21 percent of the Baptists do not; and while only 3 percent of the Episcopalians spend two or more evenings in church, 52 percent of the Southern Baptists do so. Indeed, 20 percent of the Southern Baptists typically spend *three* nights a week in church activities, and 4 percent spend *four or more* nights a week in church! Even slightly higher rates characterize participation among members of the small sects. Judged on this question, the ultra-conservative Protestant bodies are far more successful in achieving participation in church affairs than are the less conservative and liberal Protestant groups, and the Roman Catholics are less successful than any Protestant body except the Episcopalians.

These findings are confirmed and elaborated in Table 29. The first item in the table shows the total number of church organizations, groups, or activities in which members participate. Nineteen percent of all Protestants participate in three or more, while only 6 percent of the Catholics do so. Looking at the boldface figures at the bottom of the item we see that 59 percent of all the Protestants participate in at least one such activity while only 35 percent of the Catholics do so; Protestants reach a majority of their members with at least one activity, while only about a third of the Roman Catholics are similarly mobilized. Contrasts among Protestant bodies are quite great. While only 11 percent of the Episcopalians and 13 percent of the Congregationalists take part in three or more such activities, 44 percent of the Southern Baptists, and 27 percent of the sect members do so. Indeed, 10 percent of the Southern Baptists take part in at least *six* such activities!

Not only are Protestants (especially conservative ones) more likely than Catholics to take some part in church activities, they are better attenders of those activities. Twenty-three percent of the Protestants attended all of the last five meetings of each activity in which they take part, while only 9 percent of the Catholics did so. Thus Protestants not only are likely to take part in more programs of the church, they are more active in them than are the Catholics. Indeed, in no single Protestant denomina-

Table 29

PARTICIPATION IN CHURCH ORGANIZATIONS (Church-Member Sample)

"The total number of church organizations, groups, or activities participated in."

	Congre-gational	Metho-dist	Episco-palian	Disciples of Christ	Presby-terian	American Lutheran	American Baptist	Missouri Lutheran	Southern Baptist	Sects	TOTAL Protestant	Roman Catholic
Number:	(151)	(415)	(416)	(50)	(495)	(208)	(141)	(116)	(79)	(255)	(2,326)	(545)
Percentage who reported:												
Three or more	13	23	11	30	19	22	22	16	44	27	19	6
Two	18	17	11	20	18	14	23	16	15	20	16	8
One	23	20	25	26	26	25	25	28	14	23	24	21
Percentage who participated in any church organizations.	54	60	47	76	63	61	70	60	73	70	59	35

Average attendance at last five meetings of all church organizations belonged to.

	Congre-gational	Metho-dist	Episco-palian	Disciples of Christ	Presby-terian	American Lutheran	American Baptist	Missouri Lutheran	Southern Baptist	Sects	TOTAL Protestant	Roman Catholic
Percentage who reported:												
Five	17	18	19	14	24	19	30	25	33	31	23	9
Four	17	17	8	32	16	17	12	14	13	18	15	6
Three to one	15	15	10	22	14	16	19	14	15	11	15	10

tion was either participation or attendance as low as for Catholics. A partial answer to why these differences obtain may lie in the differences in the structure of Protestant and Catholic religious communities. A great deal of what could be called participation in Catholicism does not occur in direct relation to the parish church. Attending P.T.A. at the parish parochial school is as religiously involved an act as much that goes on in Protestant church organizations. Similarly many Catholic community social clubs are quite as religiously oriented and influenced as are Protestant church-sponsored social clubs. However, Catholics tend not to see these as church activities, but simply as Catholic community activities. The church is ubiquitous in affairs of the Catholic community and its presence taken for granted, while among Protestants, activities that are not church linked are typically entirely secular. To pick an extreme example, attending meetings of the American Newspaper Guild could by no stretch of definitions be called religious participation, but attending meetings of a Catholic newspaperman's association might well be. Thus, the resources for religious participation for Protestants lie mainly in the churches, while Catholics have a wide range of religious resources in the community in general. Consequently, these data on religious participation must be interpreted cautiously. The extent to which Catholics take part in religiously-oriented activities outside the immediate scope of the parish church is not reported.

Such caution does not extend to contrasts among Protestant bodies, however. It seems conclusive that the very conservative bodies get a far greater proportion of their members to take part more actively in more activities than do the liberal denominations.

Financial Support

Lacking tax support American churches rely upon the voluntary contributions of members for their funds. Commonly, contributions to the church are in the form of a public offering placed in the collection plate during worship services. Furthermore, whether one places his contributions in the collection plate or pays directly into the church treasury, pledges are solicited and checked against records of contributions. Consequently, financial contributions to the church are subject to considerable public pressure and individual accountability.

Traditionally, Christianity advocated the tithe; members were required to contribute 10 percent of their earnings to the faith. In modern times this practice has lapsed—only in very conservative bodies, particularly small sects, is the doctrine of tithing given much emphasis today. Still, churches exert considerable efforts to get maximum contributions from their members. As can be seen in Table 30, modern churches fall far short of meeting the standard of the tithe. The figures below the broken line in the table show the reported annual income of members of each of the denominations, while those above the line show their reported weekly church contributions. Given that 64 percent of the Congregationalists, for example, earn more than $10,000 a year, if they all tithed one would expect that 64 percent would report weekly church contributions of $20 a week or more. Yet only 1 percent of the Congregationalists report giving as much as $15 a week. Indeed, contributions among Protestant bodies tend to rise as their average income falls. More detailed analysis than is shown in Table 30 reveals that none of the Southern Baptists reported an income of $16,000 or more, while 23 percent of the Congregationalists did so. However, 32 percent of the Southern Baptists report giving $15 or more a week to the church, while only 1 percent of the Congregationalists contribute this much money.

Overall, Protestants give more generously to the church than do Catholics. Twenty-six percent of the Protestants report giving $7.50 or more a week to their church while only 6 percent of the Catholics give this much. Forty-nine percent of the Protestants give at least $4.00 a week, while only 22 percent of the Catholics do so. While it is true that Protestants report higher incomes than do Catholics (the median Protestant income is $9,000 a year as compared with a median income of $8,000 for Catholics) these differences are considerably smaller than the differences in the amounts contributed to church.

Table 30

CHURCH CONTRIBUTIONS AND ANNUAL INCOME (Church-Member Sample)

"What is the range of your family's weekly contribution to your church?"

	Congre-gational	Metho-dist	Episco-palian	Disciples of Christ	Presby-terian	American Lutheran	American Baptist	Missouri Lutheran	Southern Baptist	Sects	TOTAL Protestant	Roman Catholic
Number:	(151)	(415)	(416)	(50)	(495)	(208)	(141)	(116)	(79)	(255)	(2,326)	(545)
$15 or more	1%	6%	7%	12%	6%	8%	15%	8%	32%	28%	10%	2%
$7.50–$14.99	14	12	11	26	14	16	24	18	27	28	16	4
$4.00–$7.49	33	27	22	24	22	24	33	23	8	16	23	16
$1.00–$3.99	42	41	46	32	49	39	19	46	20	18	40	63
Less than $1.00	5	8	9	4	5	5	4	4	6	4	6	11
No answer	5	7	5	2	4	6	5	1	6	6	6	5
Percentage who give at least $7.50:	15	18	18	38	20	24	39	26	59	56	26	6
Members Annual Income												
$10,000 or more	64%	52%	47%	46%	48%	44%	39%	41%	26%	22%	43%	34%
$7,000–$9,000	15	26	23	26	24	24	28	29	33	30	25	28
$5,000–$6,000	10	10	13	10	11	19	16	16	17	23	15	23
$4,000 or less	6	5	10	14	12	9	10	7	14	20	11	9
No answer	5	7	7	4	5	4	7	7	10	5	6	6

Another fact that is apparent in the table is the overwhelming extent to which church members are middle class. In contrast with the general public, church members are an extraordinarily affluent group; the poor are conspicuously absent from the church rolls.[5] Even in the fundamentalist sects, traditionally thought to be the special havens of the poor, the majority of members are financially comfortable.[6]

In summary, the conservative Protestant bodies receive considerably more solid financial support from their members, and all Protestant denominations receive higher per capita contributions than does the Roman Catholic church.

Saying Grace

Thus far we have considered aspects of ritual commitment which occur within the physical confines of the church (except, of course, for "attending" to worship services on television and radio). We shall now consider an act of Christian ritual which occurs primarily in the home: saying table prayers, or grace.[7]

Illustrations of the religious home typically portray a family bowed in prayer around the table. How often is this scene actually enacted in the homes of church members? The data in Table 31 indicate that 52 percent of the Protestant church members and 44 percent of the Roman Catholics report that they say grace at least once a day. In 42 percent of the Protestant and 49 percent of the Catholic homes grace is said only on special occasions or not at all. Among conservative Protestants, however, the vast majority say grace at least once a day, and 70 percent of those who belong to the smaller Protestant sects say grace at every meal. As

[5] The incomes of church members are slightly overestimated in our data due to a slight bias in the data collection. Persons with higher incomes were slightly more likely than those with lower incomes to take part in the study. This bias, however, was far too small to vitiate the generalization that church membership is predominantly a middle-class affair.

[6] These matters will be considered in some detail in Volumes Two and Three.

[7] Saying grace is included as a ritual rather than a devotional act on the assumption that such prayers are usually recited in a group context rather than privately.

Table 31

TABLE GRACE (Church-Member Sample)

"How often, if at all, are table prayers or grace said before or after meals in your home?"

	Congre-gational	Metho-dist	Episco-palian	Disciples of Christ	Presby-terian	American Lutheran	American Baptist	Missouri Lutheran	Southern Baptist	Sects	TOTAL Protestant	Roman Catholic
Number:	(151)	(415)	(416)	(50)	(495)	(208)	(141)	(116)	(79)	(255)	(2,326)	(545)
Percentage who answered:												
At all meals.	8	16	18	22	22	29	30	41	53	70	29	22
At least once a day.	27	24	21	24	26	32	30	21	20	16	23	22
At least once a week.	6	8	6	2	5	4	8	4	1	2	5	6
Only on special oc-casions.	24	25	31	32	29	22	21	19	16	5	24	25
Never, or hardly ever.	25	26	23	18	15	13	9	16	9	5	18	24

we shall see in the next chapter, church members are much more likely to frequently say personal, private prayers than they are to say grace. Among present day church members, grace at meals is common, but hardly the rule.

The Importance of Church Membership

We shall conclude this consideration of items bearing on ritual involvement with some general estimate of how important people feel their participation in church is to them. As Table 32 shows, respondents were asked, "All in all, how important would you say your church membership is to you?" Differences among the denominations are very great. While 47 percent of the Protestants said "extremely important," 61 percent of the Catholics made this reply. Furthermore, while only 25 percent of the Congregationalists and 32 percent of the Methodists judged their church membership as "extremely important," 81 percent of the Southern Baptists and members of sects did so. Thus liberal Protestants are less likely to place extreme importance on their church membership than are Roman Catholics, while conservative Protestants are more likely to do so. Similar findings were found in the national data, although the question used is not exactly comparable. While the church-member sample was asked the importance of their church membership, respondents in the national sample were asked to rate the importance of their religion. As shown in Table 33 differences among the proportions of Protestants responding "extremely important" rise from none of the Unitarians, and 26 percent of the Congregationalists up to 69 percent of the Southern Baptists. The overall figure for Protestants is 51 percent and for Catholics, 54 percent. Thus we see that, just as in the previous table, Catholics typically place more importance on their faith than do liberal and moderate Protestants, but are less likely to do so than are conservative Protestants.

An Index of Ritual Involvement

Having examined a variety of questions we may now select several to serve as a general measure of the ritual component of religious practice. However, we must be careful to select ritual

Table 32

IMPORTANCE OF CHURCH MEMBERSHIP (Church-Member Sample)

"All in all, how important would you say your church membership is to you?"

	Congre- gational	Metho- dist	Episco- palian	Disciples of Christ	Presby- terian	American Lutheran	American Baptist	Missouri Lutheran	Southern Baptist	Sects	TOTAL Protestant	Roman Catholic
Number:	(151)	(415)	(416)	(50)	(495)	(208)	(141)	(116)	(79)	(255)	(2,326)	(545)
Percentage who answered:												
Extremely important.	25	32	44	40	44	45	52	64	81	81	47	61
Quite important.	34	35	29	56	31	35	31	24	11	13	29	20
Fairly important.	25	19	15	2	15	12	11	8	4	4	14	10
Not too important or Fairly unimportant.	13	13	11	2	7	6	5	4	4	1	9	6

Table 33
IMPORTANCE OF RELIGION (National Sample)

	"All in all, how important would you say that religion is to you?"				
	Extremely	Quite	Fairly	Not too	Not at all
Unitarian (9)	0	33	11	33	23
Congregational (44)	26	51	19	4	0
United Presbyterian (76)	36	33	20	8	4
Protestant Episcopal (57)	33	42	9	9	5
Methodist (218)	45	26	20	6	3
Presbyterian Church U.S. (40)	38	28	23	10	3
The Christian Church (42)	46	17	20	7	10
American Lutheran bodies	39	39	16	5	1
Lutheran, Missouri Synod (46)	50	33	15	3	0
Evangelical Reform (28)	46	25	21	7	0
American Baptist (92)	58	27	15	0	0
Southern Baptist (187)	69	18	10	2	1
Other Baptist bodies (92)	66	23	9	2	0
Sects (132)	68	17	14	0	0
Total Protestant (1,209)	51	26	17	4	2
Roman Catholic (507)	54	30	13	3	0

acts that are encouraged by all Christian denominations, rather than those specific to a few bodies.

Although most Protestant denominations place considerable emphasis on participation in church organizations, the Catholic subculture emphasizes similar participation outside the sphere of the parish church. However, all denominations encourage their members to say grace with their meals. Similarly, while some denominations expect frequent participation in such sacraments as Holy Communion, others do not. But all invest great importance in regular attendance at worship services. The generality of table grace and church attendance recommends them as measures of ritual involvement.

These two items were combined to construct the Ritual Index.

Persons who *both* attended church every, or nearly every, week and who said grace at least once a week were classified as high on the index. Those who reported performing either of these ritual obligations this often were scored as medium. Persons who fell short of this level of performance on both ritual acts were classified as low.

Table 34

VALIDATION OF THE RITUAL INDEX
(Church-Member Sample)

		Ritual Index		
		Low	Medium	High
Percentage who think their church membership is "extremely important" to them.	Protestant	14	38	72
	Catholic	14	53	85
Percentage who belong to at least one church organization.	Protestant	38	56	80
	Catholic	9	27	53
Percentage who attended at least three of the last five meetings of a church organization.	Protestant	20	42	62
	Catholic	6	15	31
Number of cases on which percentages are based.	Protestant	526	745	1,013
	Catholic	87	206	246

To establish the validity of the Ritual Index it was used to predict several other aspects of ritual commitment, as shown in Table 34. The first item shows that the Ritual Index is a potent predictor of feeling one's church membership is "extremely important." While only 14 percent of the Catholics and Protestants scored as low on the Ritual Index thought their church membership extremely important, 85 percent of the Catholics and 72 percent of the Protestants, who scored high on the Ritual Index, gave this response. The second and third items show that the Ritual Index is also strongly related to membership in church organizations and attendance at meetings of these organizations.

We now have some general empirical standard for estimating the ritual commitment of church members, and for examining the relative ritual involvement generated by the various Christian bodies. As the data in Table 35 indicate Catholics and Protestants are, overall, about equally likely to be ritually involved— although the Catholic church seems to have a slight advantage. However, the Catholic church does not produce as high a proportion of ritually involved members as do the Lutheran and American Baptist bodies, and all denominations fall well below the levels of commitment exhibited by Southern Baptists and the various small Protestant sects. While 46 percent of the Catholics scored high on the Ritual Index, 68 percent of the Southern Baptists and 87 percent of the sect members did so. On the other hand, the more liberal Protestant bodies are far behind in efforts to generate and maintain ritual commitment: only 22 percent of the Congregationalists, 30 percent of the Episcopalians, 32 percent of the Methodists, and 39 percent of the Presbyterians scored high.

In a sample of persons, *all* of whom were formal members of specific congregations and parishes, the Christian churches generally fail to meet the standard of universal ritual commitment; *indeed the majority of Protestants and Catholics fail to fulfill even these minimal standards of ritual commitment.*

Ritual Commitment Nationwide

To conclude this chapter we must construct a measure of ritual commitment for use in the national sample. Lacking an item on table prayers in the national study, the question "All in all, how important would you say religion is to you?" was combined with the question on the frequency of church attendance to make up the national Ritual Index. Thus, persons who judged their religion to be extremely important and who attended church weekly

Table 35

RITUAL COMMITMENT (Church-Member Sample)

	Congre-gational	Metho-dist	Episco-palian	Disciples of Christ	Presby-terian	American Lutheran	American Baptist	Missouri Lutheran	Southern Baptist	Sects	TOTAL Protestant	Roman Catholic
Number:*	(151)	(403)	(410)	(48)	(486)	(205)	(138)	(115)	(78)	(250)	(2,284)	(539)
Ritual Index												
High	22%	32%	30%	40%	39%	51%	57%	53%	68%	87%	44%	46%
Medium	42	35	40	40	36	29	30	33	26	10	33	38
Low	36	33	30	20	25	20	13	14	6	3	23	16

* Numbers include only persons scored on the index.

were classified as high on ritual involvement.[8] Persons who did either of these things were scored medium; and persons who did neither were scored low.

Table 36 shows the degree to which American Christians are ritually involved in their faith. Only a small minority (28%) of the Protestants, and fewer than half (45%) of the Catholics

Table 36
RITUAL INVOLVEMENT (National Sample)

	Low 0	Medium 1	High 2	
Unitarian (9)	89	11	0	100%
Congregational (44)	50	34	16	100%
United Presbyterian (76)	50	36	14	100%
Protestant Episcopal (57)	53	23	24	100%
Methodist (218)	48	26	26	100%
Presbyterian Church U.S. (40)	53	22	25	100%
The Christian Church (42)	48	29	23	100%
American Lutheran bodies	48	32	20	100%
Lutheran, Missouri Synod (46)	35	35	30	100%
Evangelical Reform (28)	46	25	29	100%
American Baptist (92)	28	49	23	100%
Southern Baptist (187)	26	40	34	100%
Other Baptist bodies (92)	26	43	31	100%
Sects (132)	23	30	47	100%
Total Protestant (1,209)	39	33	28	100%
Roman Catholic (507)	21	34	45	100%

qualified for a high score. Thus, the Roman Catholic church presently has more success than Protestantism generally in securing high ritual involvement from the general public, but they both fail to reach the majority. Furthermore, 39 percent of the Protestants scored low on the index, a considerably larger proportion

[8] Because attending church every week is highly correlated with saying religion is extremely important, it was decided in the absence of a more suitable alternative to include the latter item in the national index of ritual commitment.

than scored high. Twenty-one percent of the Catholics scored low. Within Protestantism there is of course great variation in the success of the various denominations in obtaining a high proportion of ritually involved members. Still, in no Protestant body are as many as half high on the index. While none of the Unitarians, 14 percent of the United Presbyterians, and 16 percent of the Congregationalists scored high, 34 percent of the Southern Baptists and 47 percent of the sect members did so. Approximately half of the persons who claimed affiliation with moderate Protestant bodies were low on the index. These findings are relatively similar to those found among church members, although, of course, the two indices are not strictly comparable because of differences on the items used to construct them. Nevertheless, like orthodoxy, ritual involvement reveals large differences in commitment among contemporary Christian bodies.

Chapter 5

RELIGIOUS PRACTICE— DEVOTIONALISM

*Do not usually pray, extempore, above eight
or ten minutes (at most) without intermission.
The Doctrines and Discipline of the
Methodist Episcopal Church South, I, 1846*

We have previously identified the devotional aspect of religious practice as personal worship of the divine, typically spontaneous and private. As opposed to the formal rites and organized social character of ritual commitment, devotionalism is informal and individual. Included here are individual acts of contemplation, study, and worship such as Bible reading and prayer.

While ritual commitment is easily, and perhaps often, feigned, it would seem pointless to perform acts of devotionalism cynically. Similarly, ritual participation may stem from many non-religious motives, but this could hardly be so of devotionalism. Thus, devotionalism seems an especially basic standard for estimating the extent of religious commitment. In what follows we shall examine a variety of devotional activities and see how successful modern churches are in obtaining such commitment from their members.

BIBLE READING

Personal Bible reading is fundamental to the Protestant tradition. In principle each Protestant is expected to be his own theologian and is charged with gaining his own scriptural understanding of the will of God. In practice, of course, Protestants mainly take their personal interpretations of scripture from that taught by their churches, but even so the tradition of personal Bible reading has remained of great importance. Among Roman Catholics, on the other hand, for centuries the laity was prevented from reading the Bible. Only in relatively recent times have Roman Catholics been permitted Bibles in their native languages and personal Bible reading is still not given much emphasis. As one Catholic respondent wrote, "For the most part Catholics do not read the Bible, it is read to them."

These differences in the emphasis given personal Bible reading are strongly reflected by the actual practices of members. As Table 37 shows, 46 percent of all Protestants are classified as "Bible readers," while only 14 percent of the Roman Catholics read the Bible with any frequency. Similarly, more than half of the Catholics (53%) reported they rarely or never read the Bible, while less than a fourth (23%) of the Protestants did so. Indeed, in *no* Protestant denomination was Bible reading so infrequent as among Catholics. Nevertheless, differences among Protestants are even greater than those between Protestants and Catholics. While 20 percent of the Congregationalists and 29 percent of the Methodists could be classified as Bible-readers, 86 percent of the Southern Baptists and 89 percent of the sect members were so classified. In fact, more than a third of these religious conservatives reported reading the Bible once or more each day. Missouri Lutherans, who on most measures have resembled the other more conservative groups, do not follow suit on Bible reading. Rather, they are like the moderate groups in the middle of the table. Overall, even occasional Bible reading is relatively rare among Roman Catholics and among members of the most liberal Protestant bodies, but it is typical of the most conservative Protestants.

PRAYER

Undoubtedly the primary private ritual expectation of Christian churches is prayer. In all denominations members are urged to use prayer as a personal means for worshipping God and for seeking divine aid and guidance. It seems likely that prayer is the most personally meaningful and rewarding of ritual acts and is the easiest to fulfill. "Of all forms of worship," a radio evangelist

Table 37

BIBLE READING (Church-Member Sample)

"How often do you read the Bible at home?"

	Congre-gational	Metho-dist	Episco-palian	Disciples of Christ	Presby-terian	American Lutheran	American Baptist	Missouri Lutheran	Southern Baptist	Sects	TOTAL Protestant	Roman Catholic
Number:	(151)	(415)	(416)	(50)	(495)	(208)	(141)	(116)	(79)	(255)	(2,326)	(545)
Percentage who answered:												
Once a day or more.	3	6	9	12	10	11	11	14	35	36	13	2
At least once a week.	4	5	4	10	13	11	15	7	28	20	11	4
Quite often but not regularly.	13	18	17	36	23	22	28	25	23	33	22	8
Percentage Bible Readers	**20**	**29**	**30**	**58**	**46**	**44**	**54**	**46**	**86**	**89**	**46**	**14**
Seldom.	47	37	36	36	31	30	39	35	10	8	30	33
Rarely or never.	33	34	32	6	21	24	16	19	3	3	23	53

once said, "prayer costs nothing, takes the least time, and does the most good." If this is true, then prayer should provide a maximum estimate of devotionalism. In the following pages we shall attempt to estimate the frequency of prayer, the importance church members attach to prayer, the uses to which prayer is put, and the extent to which it is believed to be efficacious.

As can be seen in Table 38, there is some support for the expectation that the frequency of private prayer would provide a maximum estimate of devotionalism. In the liberal denominations, on the left-hand side of the table, members are more likely to pray at least once a week than they were to attend church weekly. For example, recalling Table 24, in Chapter 4, 45 percent of the Congregationalists were weekly church attenders, while Table 38 shows that 62 percent of them report weekly prayer. Similar contrasts hold for the Methodists (51% versus 63%), Episcopalians (56% versus 72%) and so on across the table to the American Baptists. But beginning with this body the differences in the proportions reporting weekly church attendance and weekly prayer become trivial or nonexistent. Among the more conservative Protestant bodies the overwhelming majority attend church *and* pray. Seemingly conservative Protestants who are sufficiently "religious" to pray are sufficiently religious to attend church. It is only among the more liberal Protestants that persons pray frequently but are irregular attenders. It must also be noted, however, that a substantial minority of persons in the liberal bodies are as unlikely to pray as they are to attend church and thus fail to meet even the most generous criteria of religious practice.

Contrasts between Protestants and Catholics are not substantial, although Catholics are a bit more likely to report weekly prayer than are Protestants. However, similar proportions of both Protestants and Catholics (6%) report they rarely or never pray.

Private prayer, of course, can take many forms and meanings. It can consist of little more than a mechanical repetition of some formula prayer, or it can be impassioned worship. We shall now consider the nature of prayers.

Perhaps the most emphasized kind of prayer in Christianity is

Table 38

FREQUENCY OF PRAYER (Church-Member Sample)

"How often do you pray privately?"

	Congregational	Methodist	Episcopalian	Disciples of Christ	Presbyterian	American Lutheran	American Baptist	Missouri Lutheran	Southern Baptist	Sects	TOTAL Protestant	Roman Catholic
Number:	(151)	(415)	(416)	(50)	(495)	(208)	(141)	(116)	(79)	(255)	(2,326)	(545)
Percentage who answered:												
At least once a week or more.	62	63	72	82	77	75	75	82	92	92	75	83
Once in a while.	26	27	19	14	16	19	21	16	8	7	18	10
Rarely or never.	11	9	9	4	7	5	3	2	0	0	6	6

Table 39
FREQUENCY AND IMPORTANCE OF PRAYER (Church-Member Sample)

	Congregational	Methodist	Episcopalian	Disciples of Christ	Presbyterian	American Lutheran	American Baptist	Missouri Lutheran	Southern Baptist	Sects	TOTAL Protestant	Roman Catholic
Number:	(151)	(415)	(416)	(50)	(495)	(208)	(141)	(116)	(79)	(255)	(2,326)	(545)

"How often do you ask forgiveness for your sins?"
Percentage who answered:

Very often.	9	16	31	34	25	38	27	47	61	43	29	42
Quite often.	25	27	27	34	32	30	36	39	28	25	29	33
Occasionally.	30	29	24	26	25	22	26	13	9	20	24	16
Rarely.	19	17	11	4	11	5	6	1	0	7	10	5
Never.	13	9	6	0	5	5	5	1	0	2	6	3
No answer.	4	2	1	2	2	0	1	0	3	4	2	1

"How important is prayer in your life?"
Percentage who answered:

Extremely important.	32	39	50	56	51	52	54	66	85	84	53	65
Fairly important.	42	39	31	38	34	35	35	29	11	14	31	26
Not too important.	17	14	12	6	10	7	6	3	1	1	9	5
Not important.	2	3	2	0	2	1	1	1	0	0	2	1
Never pray.	7	5	5	*	4	5	4	1	3	1	4	3

* Less than half of 1%.

for the forgiveness of sins. As shown in Table 39, 58 percent of the Protestants and 75 percent of the Catholics said they ask forgiveness for their sins "very" or "quite" often. Among Protestants, Southern Baptists (89%) and Missouri Synod Lutherans (86%) are most likely to seek remission of their sins often, while 43 percent of the Methodists and 34 percent of the Congregationalists do so.

Very similar findings can be seen on the second item in the table where members were asked to evaluate the importance prayer plays in their lives. A minority of the Congregationalists (32%) and Methodists (39%) say prayer is "extremely important" in their lives, about half of those in the middle-of-the-road denominations feel prayer is extremely important to them, and the overwhelming majority of Southern Baptists (85%) and sect members (84%) give this answer. Overall about half of the Protestants (53%) and two-thirds of the Catholics (65%) said prayer was extremely important in their lives.

In summary, prayer is more common among liberal Protestants than is frequent church attendance, but prayer and attendance are equally common among conservative Protestants. Roman Catholics place more importance upon prayer, and are more likely to pray frequently than are Protestants in general, but conservative Protestants surpass Catholics in their prayerfulness.

We may now examine the reasons for prayer. Respondents were asked, "When you pray, why do you pray?" The ten reasons provided respondents are presented in Table 40, ranked from the most to the least chosen. In general it may be said that Protestants and Catholics are extremely similar in the reasons they give for praying. Both were most likely to say they pray "To give thanks to God" (85% and 84% respectively) and least likely to say they pray "As a Christian duty" (22% and 30%). About three-fourths of each group said they prayed "To ask God's guidance in making decisions." On most items differences among Protestant bodies are not nearly as great as we have seen on other ritual practices or on religious beliefs. Indeed, the differences that are shown stem mainly from the fact that many fewer persons in the liberal denominations gave *any* reason for praying than in the more conservative bodies. Since a significant minority of the liberal Protestants rarely or never pray they could hardly be expected to give reasons for their prayers. Among persons who do pray with some frequency, however, persons in both liberal and conservative Protestant bodies reported similar reasons for doing so.

To further investigate the reasons for prayer, respondents were asked about a variety of prayers of petition. As can be seen in Table 41, 42 percent of both Protestants and Roman Catholics said that at some time during their adult years they had prayed "to ask God to restore my health." An even greater proportion, 79 percent of the Protestants and 78 percent of the Catholics say they have prayed "To ask God to restore someone else's health." Indeed, in *every* denomination a large majority have prayed for someone else's health.

Forty-eight percent of the Protestants and 59 percent of the Catholics said they had prayed "To ask God to keep some misfortune from happening to me." It must be kept in mind, however, that respondents were asked if they had *ever* prayed for any of these reasons, thus the data indicate that the majority of Christian church members report that they have *never* prayed about their health, and a near majority have never prayed to avoid misfortunes. Moreover, only 12 percent of the Protestants and 21 percent of the Catholics indicate they have *ever* prayed "To ask for some material thing, for example, a new car or a new house." Despite the fact that one of our respondents wrote that she had "practically furnished" her "whole house through prayer," Christians generally do not use prayer for these purposes. However, members of small sects are much more likely than are other Christians to pray for consumer goods—30 percent reported doing so.

The Efficacy of Prayer

We have seen thus far that American denominations differ greatly in the extent to which their members engage in and are committed to prayer. Frequent prayer is the overwhelming norm among members of the conservative Protestant bodies and among

Table 40

THE REASONS FOR PRAYER (Church-Member Sample)

"When you pray, why do you pray?" (Check as many as apply.)

	Congre-gational	Metho-dist	Episco-palian	Disciples of Christ	Presby-terian	American Lutheran	American Baptist	Missouri Lutheran	Southern Baptist	Sects	TOTAL Protestant	Roman Catholic
Number:	(151)	(415)	(416)	(50)	(495)	(208)	(141)	(116)	(79)	(255)	(2,326)	(545)
Percentage who answered:												
To give thanks to God.	72	80	83	94	86	88	81	91	94	95	85	84
To ask God's guidance in making decisions.	70	72	70	90	77	80	83	84	92	93	78	71
To ask forgiveness for something I have done.	44	57	62	72	65	68	74	78	91	86	65	68
To find comfort when I am feeling low.	58	61	56	70	60	65	65	66	84	84	63	62
To strengthen my faith.	39	43	49	74	55	63	64	69	78	85	57	55

Because it gives me a feeling of being closer to God.	40	47	44	62	53	51	60	59	84	83	54	54
To try to learn God's will.	42	42	47	70	51	45	65	49	77	82	53	39
To be worshipful of God.	28	37	40	60	43	48	53	54	72	79	47	53
To ask God to bring someone else to Christian faith and belief.	21	25	26	38	33	42	51	48	87	87	40	37
As a Christian duty.	12	11	24	16	17	23	24	21	28	48	22	30

Table 41

PRAYING FOR HEALTH, WEALTH, AND GOOD FORTUNE (Church-Member Sample)

"Have you ever prayed during your adult years for the following purposes?" (Check each you have done.)

	Congregational	Methodist	Episcopalian	Disciples of Christ	Presbyterian	American Lutheran	American Baptist	Missouri Lutheran	Southern Baptist	Sects	TOTAL Protestant	Roman Catholic
Number:	(151)	(415)	(416)	(50)	(495)	(208)	(141)	(116)	(79)	(255)	(2,326)	(545)
Percentage who answered:												
To ask God to restore my health.	23	29	40	48	44	47	36	52	49	71	42	42
To ask God to restore someone else's health.	68	73	81	84	78	78	78	84	87	92	79	78
To ask God to keep some misfortune from happening to me.	37	39	51	44	47	54	50	58	47	59	48	59
To ask for some material thing, for example, a new car or a new house.	5	7	10	12	10	12	15	14	11	30	12	21

Table 42

EFFICACY OF PRAYER (Church-Member Sample)

	Congregational	Methodist	Episcopalian	Disciples of Christ	Presbyterian	American Lutheran	American Baptist	Missouri Lutheran	Southern Baptist	Sects	TOTAL Protestant	Roman Catholic
Number:	(151)	(415)	(416)	(50)	(495)	(208)	(141)	(116)	(79)	(255)	(2,326)	(545)

"Do you feel your prayers are answered?"
Percentage who answered:

Yes, I have no doubt that they are.	43	47	57	58	62	67	63	74	87	85	61	70

"How certain are you your sins are forgiven?"
Percentage who answered:

Absolutely certain.	14	25	29	32	37	47	47	66	87	84	42	57
Fairly certain.	27	23	23	26	22	23	19	16	6	9	20	18
Sometimes, but not always.	9	12	13	16	12	10	13	9	4	4	10	9
I am never quite sure.	13	14	14	14	12	12	7	7	1	1	10	8
I don't think of sin in this way.	32	24	19	8	14	8	11	2	0	1	14	6
No answer.	5	2	1	4	4	0	13	1	1	1	2	2

Roman Catholics, but the majority of persons in the more liberal Protestant denominations pray infrequently. We shall now examine the confidence Christians place in prayer.

Looking at Table 42 it is apparent that Christians are not unanimous in believing their prayers are answered. Overall, less than two-thirds of the Protestants (61%) and 70 percent of the Catholics are certain that their prayers are answered. In contrast with the respondent who wrote, "I am sure my prayers are always answered, but sometimes the answer is 'No,'" a great number of church members do not have unqualified faith in their prayers. In fact, less than half of the Congregationalists and Episcopalians are sure their prayers are answered. On the other hand, 74 percent of the Missouri Lutherans, 85 percent of those who belong to small sects, and 87 percent of the Southern Baptists are certain that their prayers *are* answered.

Following the question shown in Table 39, which asked how often church members asked forgiveness for their sins, they were asked, "How certain are you your sins are forgiven?" Here again enormous differences were found among Protestant denominations in the proportions who were certain of the efficacy of prayer. While 14 percent of the Congregationalists and 25 percent of the Methodists were "absolutely certain" that their sins were forgiven, 66 percent of the Missouri Lutherans, 84 percent of the sect members, and 87 percent of the Southern Baptists were without the slightest doubt. Overall, 42 percent of the Protestants and 57 percent of the Roman Catholics were absolutely certain that their sins were forgiven. Thus more than half of the Protestants and nearly half of the Catholics had some doubts about the forgiveness of their sins. An additional 20 percent of the Protestants and 18 percent of the Catholics, however, were "fairly certain" that their sins were forgiven. Still, about one-third of the Protestants and a quarter of the Catholics doubted that their sins were forgiven, or did not think of sin in terms of any divine forgiveness.

Thus, Christians vary in their certainty that prayer is efficacious—a majority are convinced but a substantial minority doubt the power of prayer.

MEASURING DEVOTIONALISM [1]

To conclude this chapter we must select means for constructing an empirical measure of devotionalism from the data presented earlier. The two most generally applicable items were selected: "How often do you pray privately?" and "How important is prayer in your life?" Respondents were scored as high on the Devotionalism Index if they felt prayer was "Extremely" impor-

Table 43

VALIDATION OF THE DEVOTIONALISM INDEX
(Church-Member Sample)

| | | Devotionalism Index | | |
		Low	Medium	High
Percentage who "ask forgiveness" for their sins "very" or "quite often."	Protestants	17	53	80
	Catholics	25	64	91
Percentage who are "Bible readers."	Protestants	9	32	70
	Catholics	0	8	19
Number of cases on which percentages are based.	Protestants	450	605	1,172
	Catholics	25	109	344

tant in their lives *and* if they prayed privately once a week or oftener. Respondents were scored medium if they met either of these criteria of devotionalism, and were scored low if they fell below both of these standards.

Table 43 tests the validity of the Devotionalism Index. The first two lines in the table show the index is a very strong predic-

[1] No questions pertaining to devotionalism were included in the national study. Consequently, it is possible to develop a general measure of devotionalism only for the church-member sample.

tor of how often respondents ask forgiveness for their sins. The proportions who say they ask forgiveness very or quite often rise from 17 percent among those Protestants scored low on the index up to 80 percent of those scored high. Among Catholics these same comparisons are 25 percent and 91 percent. The lower two lines in the table give further confidence of its validity as a sensitive measure of devotionalism. Here it strongly predicts Bible reading among both Protestants and Catholics despite the fact that few Catholics are regular Bible readers. These data also demonstrate why Bible reading was not included in the index—it would have biased the estimates of Catholic devotionalism.

Table 44 contrasts the denominations on the Devotionalism Index. As would be expected, the proportion high on the index increases greatly from the more liberal Protestant bodies on the left to the more conservative on the right. While Catholics surpass the overall Protestant figures, they fall below the Southern Baptists and the sects and closely approximate the Missouri Lutherans. Overall, these data indicate that Protestant denominations on the left are divided into thirds among high, medium, and low commitment. Denominations such as the Presbyterians obtain a high devotional commitment from about half of their members, Roman Catholics from about two-thirds, and the Southern Baptists and the various sects obtain this level of commitment from more than 80 percent of their members.

Earlier in this chapter we suggested that it was possible for ritual participation to stem from unreligious motives, but that such a possibility seems remote for devotional commitment. It seems hard to imagine a person engaging in private prayers who lacks all religious motive. Consequently, a comparison between ritual commitment and devotionalism can be extremely revealing. This comparison can only be made roughly since the indexes are not equivalent. Judging both from the indexes and the individual items, however, a conclusion is warranted that in all Protestant denominations devotionalism is more often practiced than ritual. Thus, while some people could feign religiousness through ritual participation, these differences suggest that few do so. Rather, the Protestant churches generate greater private than public

Table 44

DEVOTIONALISM (Church-Member Sample)

	Congre-gational	Metho-dist	Episco-palian	Disciples of Christ	Presby-terian	American Lutheran	American Baptist	Missouri Lutheran	Southern Baptist	Sects	TOTAL Protestant	Roman Catholic
Number:*	(140)	(390)	(394)	(50)	(477)	(196)	(136)	(115)	(77)	(252)	(2,227)	(527)
Devotionalism Index												
High	32	39	50	54	49	53	51	63	85	83	53	65
Medium	37	29	28	30	32	28	31	23	10	12	27	21
Low	31	32	22	16	19	19	18	14	5	5	20	14
	100%	100%	100%	100%	100%	100%	100%	100%	100%	100%	100%	100%

* Number includes only persons scored on the index.

religious practice. Among Catholics, however, the differences are in the other direction. Catholics are more likely to exhibit public than private religious practice. This perhaps is partly due to the heavy emphasis placed on ritual commitment by the Catholic church.

In conclusion, the major finding of this chapter is that despite the greater relative success of all Protestant bodies in gaining private rather than public religious practice, the differences in the extent to which their members are devotionally committed to religion varies greatly. Here too the notion of a common Protestant orientation is revealed as fictional.

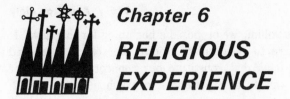

Chapter 6

RELIGIOUS EXPERIENCE

And it shall come to pass in the last days, said God, I will pour out of my Spirit upon all flesh: and your sons and your daughters shall prophesy, and your young men shall see visions, and your old men shall dream dreams:
Acts 2:17 (A.V.)

Although religious belief, ritual, and devotion have been little studied by modern social science, religious experience has been absolutely neglected. At the turn of the century, the phenomenon of religious experience engaged the interest of a number of eminent scholars, among them James Leuba,[1] Edwin Diller Starbuck,[2] and, of course, William James.[3] Since then the subject has languished.

In terms of the analytic scheme outlined in Chapter 1, religious experiences constitute one of the generic criteria for classifying and measuring religious commitment. To a greater or lesser extent all known religious institutions have some expectation that the properly religious person will at one time or another achieve some sense of contact, however vague or fleeting, with a supernatural agency. Used in this sense, the term religious experience covers an exceedingly disparate array of events: from the vaguest glimmerings of something sacred to rapturous mystical unions with the divine. Clearly some basic elements must be systematically extracted from these diverse phenomena if they are to be discussed with any conceptual quality.[4]

[1] James H. Leuba, *The Psychology of Religious Mysticism* (New York: Harcourt, Brace, 1925).

[2] Edwin Diller Starbuck, *The Psychology of Religion* (New York: Charles Scribner's Sons, 1899).

[3] William James, *The Varieties of Religious Experience* (New York: Mentor Books, 1958; first published in 1902).

[4] Despite the considerable work done on this topic several generations ago, no satisfactory conceptual scheme was produced. Although James gave a

In a previous volume we proposed a beginning for this task.[5] It is necessary here to recapitulate briefly the set of types and ordering dimensions that constitute our conceptual scheme for organizing the variety of experiences to which men attach religious definitions.

As we use the term, all religious experiences, from the vaguest to the most frenzied, *constitute occasions defined by those undergoing them as an encounter—some sense of contact—between themselves and some supernatural consciousness.*[6] In our earlier essay we suggested treating these as inter-"personal" encounters, and we attempted to show in some detail that an important dimension along which these encounters can be ordered is the

bit of attention to what class of things he meant to consider as religious experiences, he made little systematic attempt to classify these disparate psychological events. For the most part he accepted the categories which occur in the natural religious language: conversion, mysticism, and the like. His only original addition was to distinguish between religious experiences emanating from "sick" and "healthy souls." However, aside from these primitive "source" categories, his lectures were mainly devoted to a detailed recounting of individual reports of religious experiences. Leuba was only concerned with religious ecstasy, particularly "extravagant instances," and drew most of his material from case studies of the lives of saints. While the experiences of such dedicated religious adepts are a fruitful source of data, we must surely also give attention to the more ordinary experiences of more ordinary persons. Starbuck's classic work, based on one of the earliest surveys ever conducted, dealt solely with conversion among American Protestants. While conversion is likely an important kind of religious experience, any general treatment must take into account a much broader array of phenomena. The only other significant writings on religious experience are the autobiographical and biographical accounts of mystics. While Leuba and James demonstrated that these materials contain valuable data, they can hardly be expected to yield a sophisticated conceptual scheme.

[5] Charles Y. Glock and Rodney Stark, *Religion and Society in Tension* (Chicago: Rand McNally, 1965), ch. 3.

[6] It is crucial that the reader keep in mind that our formulation rests upon the subjective definitions people place on certain feelings, sensations, visions, and the like. The question of whether they are responding to some "real" stimulus—that is, actually in contact with some supernatural consciousness—or whether the experience is totally illusory, is completely irrelevant to the definition. For the actor the subjective experience is the same whatever an investigator may postulate about its sources.

sense of intimacy between the two "persons" involved. By conceiving of the divinity and the individual undergoing the religious experience as a pair of actors involved in a social encounter, we may specify some general configurations of relations between them which can be ordered in terms of social distance. Four general types of religious experience were postulated:

1. *The Confirming type:* The human actor simply notes (feels, senses, etc.) the existence or presence of the supernatural actor, but the supernatural is not perceived as specifically acknowledging the human actor.

2. *The Responsive type:* Mutual presence is acknowledged, the supernatural actor is believed to specifically note (respond to) the presence of the human actor.

3. *The Ecstatic type:* The awareness of mutual presence is replaced by an affective relationship akin to love or friendship.

4. *The Revelational type:* The human actor perceives himself as becoming a confidant of and/or a fellow participant in action with the supernatural actor.

Within each of these types several sub-types were specified. Of these, only two sub-varieties of the Responsive type need concern us here:

a. *The Salvational:* being acknowledged as especially virtuous, "chosen," "elect," or "saved" by the divine actor.

b. *The Sanctioning:* experiencing the displeasure of the supernatural actor; to be chastised or punished by the supernatural.

The primary feature of this conceptual scheme is order. The underlying assumption on which the types were developed was that religious experience is a systematically progressive phenomenon; that the diverse instances when men believe they have encountered the divine follow a patterned sequence. This development was likened to the pattern through which normal interpersonal relations build up along a continuum of increasing intimacy. It was recognized that such development could be arrested anywhere along the way, but however much men may differ in the degree of intimacy they experience with supernatural agencies, they generally start at the same place and move along the same route.

As was pointed out in the earlier volume, this ordering of religious experiences into a series of generic intervals along a dimension of intimacy coincides with the order suggested by several other criteria, including the normative definitions attached to the various types by both religious and secular standards. Nevertheless, the case for this order must rest primarily on statistical grounds. If religious experience is a unidimensional phenomenon in the manner specified, then the relative frequency with which the various types occur in the population must decrease from the less to the more intimate varieties. Similarly, men who have experienced more intimate types should have undergone the less intimate. Furthermore, the relative frequency of the types should decrease within the experience of individuals. That is, men who periodically undergo several varieties of religious experience should manifest the less intimate more frequently than, and prior to ever experiencing, the more intimate. Of these various tests of the postulated order, the last two cannot be assessed with the data at hand. Since respondents were not asked to date the first occasion of any particular religious encounter, the case will have to rest on the relative frequency of types within the sample and by determining that persons who report more intimate experiences also report the less intimate varieties. The data we shall examine to determine whether or not such an assumption of order is warranted will also enable us to get some estimate of how common religious experience is among Christian church members in contemporary America.

Before proceeding to this examination, several remarks must be made about the quality and form of the data. No questions on religious experience were included in the national study. The materials available on religious experience in the church-member study are of two sorts. Several structured questions asked respondents whether or not they had undergone various kinds of religious experiences. In addition, an open-end question sought voluntary reports of religious experience, some of which were quoted in the earlier essay. The open-end data are rich in detail, but are badly incomplete. Although they are probably reliable as far as they go, there is no way of knowing what additional experiences were omitted from these reports since the space provided was limited and respondents were not asked for a complete recounting of all incidents. Thus, many who wrote about being saved may also have had confirming or ecstatic experiences, for example, which were omitted. In examining the questionnaires, many instances were discovered when experiences acknowledged in the structured items were not mentioned in the free response. Indeed, unless respondents had been attempting to be definitive, and also shared our definition of what should be considered a religious experience, there is no reason to expect the open-end responses to provide adequate data. For these reasons, the open-end data seem best suited to provide qualitative materials on religious experience, and are of little use for quantitative purposes.

The structured items avoid this incompleteness, but are inadequate in another way. For the varieties of religious experience to which they were directed, the structured items required respondents to indicate whether or not they had ever undergone such an encounter with the supernatural, and, thus, provide a basis for classifying all respondents. But not all of the types of religious experience postulated were explored by structured items. No items were included which tap the Ecstatic, or the Revelational types.

One reason for these omissions (aside from the fact that the lack of a clear conceptual scheme at the time the data were collected made the choice of items on religious experience somewhat fortuitous) was that it was little imagined how frequently modern Christians would report religious experiences. Items aimed at the more complex and intimate types of religious encounters seemed, then, as too extreme to be credible. Given these limits on both kinds of data, the burden of the analysis will have to rest on the structured items and thus our quest to understand religious experience will be limited to the confirming and responsive varieties. The question of the frequency of these types of religious experience may now be taken up.

One such structured item in the questionnaire is a straightforward inquiry about Confirming experiences—an awareness of the presence of divinity. Respondents were asked whether they had ever, as adults, had "A feeling that they were somehow in the presence of God."

Looking at the data in Table 45 we may see how commonly American Christians have undergone Confirming experiences. Forty-five percent of the Protestants and 43 percent of the Roman Catholics reported they were "sure" they had experienced such a feeling of divine presence. Additionally, 28 percent of the Protestants and 23 percent of the Roman Catholics thought they had had such an encounter. Among Protestants, the proportions vary considerably. Twenty-five percent of the Congregationalists and 36 percent of the Methodists, are sure they have felt in the presence of God, while 80 percent of the Southern Baptists and 75 percent of the sect members are sure. Overall, more than two-thirds of the Christian church members in this sample at least thought they'd had a confirming experience, and nearly half were certain of it.

The absolute frequency of even this least intimate variety of religious experience seems something of a surprise. There are few cues in the culture which would lead an observer to predict so high a rate of supernaturalism in what seems to be an increasingly modern, scientific, and secularized society. For example, characters in contemporary literature rarely undergo such encounters with the divine, and when they do it is usually clear that they are odd people, old-fashioned, simple, demented, and the like. Furthermore, a recent Gallup survey of a national sample of Americans found only 20 percent felt they had undergone a religious experience of some variety.[7] Of these, most were of the Confirming variety. The great discrepancy between Gallup's findings and those we are now examining must be in part produced by differences in the populations sampled. While about one-fifth of the

---

[7] American Institute of Public Opinion, poll of April, 1962. One source of difference between our findings and Gallup's is undoubtedly in the way the questions were asked. Gallup merely asked if people had ever had a religious experience, and did not define what he meant by this term. Our items, by posing a series of occurrences which we regard as religious experiences, are more apt to elicit fuller reporting.

Table 45

CONFIRMING EXPERIENCES (Church-Member Sample)

"A feeling that you were somehow in the presence of God."

	Congregational	Methodist	Episcopal	Disciples of Christ	Presbyterian	American Lutheran	American Baptist	Missouri Lutheran	Southern Baptist	Sects	TOTAL Protestant	Roman Catholic
Number:	(151)	(415)	(416)	(50)	(495)	(208)	(141)	(116)	(79)	(255)	(2,326)	(545)
Percentage who answered:												
Yes, I'm sure I have.	25	36	42	48	42	39	50	49	80	75	45	43
Yes, think that I have.	37	34	28	26	30	27	27	31	14	15	28	23
No.	30	24	25	14	20	25	15	16	0	5	20	25
Did not answer.	8	6	5	12	8	9	8	4	6	5	7	9

general population report divine encounters, these proportions increase greatly among a population drawn entirely from members of Christian churches. This strongly suggests that having such an encounter is intimately connected with participation in religious situations. We shall take up this question later, but in any event it is clear from the data in Table 45 that an investigation of religious experience among Christian church members is not a quest to understand a rare phenomenon. For all that religious experiences may be strange, they are not unusual. Indeed, *most* of the persons in our sample at least thought they might have undergone a confirming encounter with the Divine.

We have earlier postulated that Confirming experiences are more common than Responsive experiences. The data in Table 46 lend some support to this assumption. In all but the more conservative Protestant bodies, Responsive experiences of both the Salvational and Sanctioning variety were considerably less often reported than were Confirming experiences. Among the conservative Protestant groups, however, Salvational experiences were about as widespread as Confirming, although Sanctioning experiences were much less common than were the Confirming. One reason for this is that both Confirming and Salvational experiences were so widespread in these groups that it was virtually impossible for there to be any differences. But more importantly, these bodies (sects, Southern Baptists, etc.) place enormous emphasis on personal experiences of being saved. Indeed, in many sects elaborate formal ceremonies are conducted to produce such contacts with the divine and one does not qualify for membership in the congregation until such an experience has been accomplished. In general, however, Responsive experiences are less common than are the Confirming variety.

The data also reveal some interesting contrasts between Protestants and Roman Catholics. To seek an experience affirming one's salvation is a much more familiar part of the rhetoric of Protestantism than of Catholicism. This difference in emphasis is reflected in the data. Thirty-seven percent of the Protestants were certain they had had "A sense of being saved in Christ," while only 26 percent of the Roman Catholics were certain they had

Table 46
RESPONSIVE EXPERIENCES (Church-Member Sample)

	Congre- gational	Metho- dist	Episco- pal	Disciples of Christ	Presby- terian	American Lutheran	American Baptist	Missouri Lutheran	Southern Baptist	Sects	TOTAL Protestant	Roman Catholic
Number:	(151)	(415)	(416)	(50)	(495)	(208)	(141)	(116)	(79)	(255)	(2,326)	(545)
SALVATIONAL												
"A sense of being saved in Christ."												
Percentage who an- swered:												
Yes, I'm sure I have.	9	18	20	34	31	37	56	52	92	85	37	26
Yes, I think that I have.	19	28	24	38	27	25	20	31	5	9	23	22
SANCTIONING												
"A feeling of being punished by God for something you had done."												
Percentage who an- swered:												
Yes, I'm sure I have.	5	11	14	8	13	20	13	27	47	25	16	23
Yes, I think that I have.	25	20	27	22	26	24	28	32	28	24	25	30

done so. An additional 23 percent of the Protestants and 22 percent of the Catholics thought they had had such a sense of salvation.

Looking at the second item in the table, Sanctioning experiences, the Catholics seem much more consistent than the Protestants. Many fewer Protestants were sure they had had a "Feeling of being punished by God for something you had done," than reported a Salvational experience. Catholics reported Sanctioning experiences virtually as frequently as they reported the Salvational. Hence, while 37 percent of the Protestants were certain they had had a salvational experience, only 16 percent were sure they had been Sanctioned. The same comparison among Catholics is 26 percent versus 23 percent. These contrasts seem to match differences in the conceptions of God held by Protestants and Catholics. For many Protestants God seems endlessly benevolent—indeed, many Protestants believe in heaven, but deny there is a hell—while the Catholic God is more often depicted as a judge who punishes as well as rewards and virtually all Catholics in this sample who believed there was a heaven also believed in hell. In any event, either sub-type of Responsive experience, as expected, is less frequently reported than are Confirming experiences.

Table 47 gives further statistical support for the proposed ordering of the types. Of those persons who were sure they had had a Salvational experience, 81 percent were certain they had undergone a Confirming experience, and an additional 15 percent thought they had done so. Thus, 96 percent of those who reported a Salvational experience acknowledged a Confirming experience. Seen in reverse, however, many who reported a Confirming experience *did not* also report a Salvational experience (only 66% were certain they had had one). This increases the confidence which may be placed in the hypothesis that the manifestation of the more intimate types of religious experience presupposes previous encounters of a less intimate variety.

Aside from theoretical considerations, this confirmation is methodologically fortunate. For implicit in the discussion of the ordering of types was the expectation that religious experience

Table 47

VIRTUALLY ALL WHO REPORTED A SALVATIONAL
EXPERIENCE REPORTED A CONFIRMING EXPERIENCE *

	"Since you have been an adult have you ever had . . . a sense of being saved in Christ?"		
	"Yes, I'm sure I have."	"Yes, I think that I have."	"No."
"Since you have been an adult have you ever had a feeling that you were somehow in the presence of God?"			
Percentage who responded:			
Yes, I'm sure I have.	81	36	20
Yes, I think that I have.	15	50	27
No.	4	14	53
	100%	100%	100%
Number	(941)	(642)	(850)

* Persons who failed to respond to either item have been omitted.

has a cumulative or scalar quality; that encounters with the supernatural follow a developmental sequence along a single dimension. These data display this hypothesized scalar character.

Given this outcome, we may briefly discuss the summary measure, or index, of religious experience that will serve as the basis for subsequent analysis. The three items discussed above were used to classify respondents through a simple indexing procedure.[8] In the subsequent analysis, initially the index was used in its original form, ranging respondents from a score of zero (earned by answering "No" to all three questions) to six (earned by answering "Yes, I'm sure I have" to all three). These tables revealed that all the relationships were isotropic—no matter what cutting points were chosen to collapse the index the direction of relationship was unchanged—hence, the index was collapsed into

[8] A score of 2 was given for each response of "Yes, I'm sure I have"; a score of 1 for each response of "Yes, I think that I have" and zero for each response of "No." Persons who failed to answer any of the three items were not indexed.

three categories for ease in presentation. The first category, High, contains all respondents who *at least* answered "Yes, I think that I have," to all three questions (combining scores of 3 through 6). The Medium category contains persons who thought they might have had one or two of these experiences (scores of 1 or 2). The None group includes only persons who were certain that they had *not* had any of these experiences.

Turning to the data in Table 48, we may see that the propensity for religious encounters is greatly influenced by the denomination to which a person belongs. While 24 percent of the Congregationalists are classified as high on the index of religious experience, 76 percent of the Missouri Synod Lutherans, 94 percent of those in sects, and 97 percent of the Southern Baptists scored high. Religious experience increases systematically from the more liberal groups on the left of the table to the more conservative groups on the right.

Overall, there seems to be little difference between Protestants and Catholics. While 58 percent of the Protestants are high on the index, 57 percent of the Catholics are high. Yet the data show how fictional it is to rely on only such comparisons, for the majority of Protestant denominations diverge greatly from the picture presented by the total Protestant figures. Only four of the ten groups could be said to be fairly represented by the overall figures. This massive discrepancy between the "average" Protestants and specific denominations was also reported in the preceding chapters on religious beliefs and on religious rituals. These findings suggest once again that the typical Protestant-Catholic comparisons, on which most of the empirical literature in the study of religion are based, are worse than futile, they may have been positively pernicious in their influence upon our judgments of social realities.

Before concluding this chapter, one further matter must be considered. Thus far we have only discussed experiences with a "good" supernatural consciousness; however, the voluminous reports of satanic encounters—including such famous incidents as the incubi attacks on the nuns of Loudon [9] or Martin Luther's

[9] See: Aldous Huxley, *The Devils of Loudon* (New York: Harpers, 1952).

Table 48

RELIGIOUS EXPERIENCE (Church-Member Sample)

	Congre-gational	Metho-dist	Episco-palian	Disciples of Christ	Presby-terian	American Lutheran	American Baptist	Missouri Lutheran	Southern Baptist	Sects	TOTAL Protestant	Roman Catholic
Number:*	(119)	(325)	(341)	(39)	(403)	(169)	(117)	(211)	(78)	(211)	(1,875)	(422)
Index of Religious Experience												
High	24%	40%	50%	52%	56%	61%	74%	76%	97%	94%	58%	57%
Medium	48	42	30	34	30	31	17	21	3	6	28	25
None	28	18	20	14	14	8	9	3	0	0	14	18

* Persons who failed to answer any of the three questions on religious experience were dropped from the analysis.

violent engagements with a variety of devils [10]—suggest that, historically, "evil" and "good" supernatural forces have both been commonly encountered. Simply to keep these two kinds of encounters separate we shall speak of *divine* and *diabolic* religious experiences. Because there seem to be reasonable grounds for asserting that diabolic contacts have played nearly as important a role as the divine in Western religious life, any attempt to study religious experience ought to consider both kinds of supernatural agents.

The conceptual scheme presented in our previous essay directly adapted the types developed for contact with the divine to classify contacts with the diabolic. However, only one question on encounters with the Devil was asked of our respondents. This question fits what we have called the Temptational type which directly corresponds to the Salvational sub-type of Responsive experiences with the divine. Looking at the data in Table 49 it is clear that the Temptational experience is about as common as the Salvational among contemporary Christian church members. Thirty-two percent of the Protestants said they were "sure" they had had a feeling as adults "of being tempted by the Devil" (37% were sure they had been saved). Temptational experiences are even more commonly reported by Catholics than are Salvational: 36 percent of the Catholics were sure they had been tempted by the Devil, while only 26 percent were equally sure they had been saved. In addition, 20 percent of the Protestants and 26 percent of the Catholics thought they had had such a satanic encounter. Thus, well over half of these modern Christians at least thought they had been tempted by the Devil. As would be anticipated, the differences among the Protestant bodies are enormous. While only 11 percent of the Congregationalists said they were sure they had been tempted, 50 percent of the Missouri Lutherans, 68 percent of the sect members, and 76 percent of the Southern Baptists were sure. Similarly, only a quarter of the Congregationalists as much

[10] This important aspect of Luther's life and character, largely ignored in the vast literature about this great Protestant, is treated sensitively by Erik H. Erikson, in his *Young Man Luther* (New York: W. W. Norton, 1962).

Table 49

TEMPTATIONAL EXPERIENCES (Church-Member Sample)

"A feeling of being tempted by the Devil."

	Congre-gational	Metho-dist	Episco-palian	Disciples of Christ	Presby-terian	American Lutheran	American Baptist	Missouri Lutheran	Southern Baptist	Sects	TOTAL Protestant	Roman Catholic
Number:	(151)	(415)	(416)	(50)	(495)	(208)	(141)	(116)	(79)	(255)	(2,326)	(545)
Percentage who an-swered:												
Yes, I'm sure I have.	11	16	24	24	24	41	36	50	76	68	32	36
Yes, I think I have.	14	16	19	24	22	21	24	32	22	19	20	26

as thought they had been tempted, while an overwhelming 98 percent of the Southern Baptists at least thought so. Thus, the vast majority of persons in the liberal Protestant bodies seem to lead relatively unbedeviled lives, but the average conservative Protestant feels himself confronted by evil forces beckoning him from the paths of righteousness.

Further analysis showed that diabolic experiences, at least as measured by this single item, were extremely correlated with the Index of Religious Experiences made up of items based on encounters with the Divine. Consequently, it will be unnecessary to treat divine and diabolic experiences separately and the single index will suffice for future analysis.

Chapter 7

RELIGIOUS KNOWLEDGE

Go ye therefore, and teach all nations. . . .
Matthew 28:19 (A.V.)

It is obvious that some minimum of knowledge is necessary for religious commitment; the tenets and rituals of a religion must be known if they are to be believed and practiced. Yet it is equally obvious that beliefs may be held in virtual ignorance and rituals practiced blindly, they may be solemnly adhered to but not understood. Thus, all religious institutions expect their members to know more than doctrine and ritual, they expect a certain amount of comprehension. Furthermore, all religions expect properly committed members to be informed on matters beyond the simplest beliefs and practices, to know something of the history, traditions, and in literate societies, the scriptures of the faith.

Before turning to the data some general remarks are necessary about the nature of the questions we used to measure religious knowledge. To most readers the questions we asked will seem extremely obvious and easy. Indeed, several theologians who assisted us in fashioning the questionnaire felt that to use these questions to measure religious knowledge is a travesty on the meaning of knowledge and to speak of them as assessing the degree to which people have grasped the cultural heritage of their faith demeans that heritage. From the point of view of a sophisticated person we readily admit that the items used in this chapter touch only the most obvious portions of the Christian cultural heritage. And indeed they do not reflect our own conception of what it means to be highly knowledgeable about religion. But if we had used more sophisticated items we would not be able to study variations in religious knowledge among rank-and-file Christians, for virtually no one in our sample would have been able to answer them. What point, for example, would there be in asking people to recount and interpret the Sermon on the Mount, when more than *two-thirds* of American Christians do not even know who delivered this sermon? (See Table 57 below.)

This is a problem survey researchers have long lived with. If we construct a set of items that will be of any practical use in measuring the average person's knowledge about virtually anything, we are often abused for *our* simplemindedness. But this apparent simplemindedness is imposed upon us by the realities of the prevailing level of public ignorance. Unless we are willing to give up the study of the general public, and give our attention to samples restricted to college students or intellectuals, we must confront people with relatively easy knowledge questions. But, we would argue that to know this is in itself a major contribution made by survey research to an understanding of our society. If our questions seem trivial, we ask you to notice how few people could answer them correctly.

It is in these terms, then, that we examine in this chapter the success of contemporary Christianity in transmitting its cultural heritage to its members. In so doing we shall seek criteria for classifying persons according to the degree they satisfy this intellectual aspect of religious commitment.

THE TEN COMMANDMENTS

The most revered moral statement in Judeo-Christian culture is the Ten Commandments, the set of laws believed to have been dictated to Moses on Mount Sinai by God himself. If this code is not universally practiced, it is certainly universally preached. The rote learning of these brief statements is the common denominator of all Christian and Jewish religious education. They are something everybody knows. But is this really true?

To try to learn the answer to this question, we decided to ask respondents to assess their own knowledge. In an effort to overcome the propensity of people to claim more knowledge than they actually have, the item was designed to make it as easy as possible to admit ignorance:

"If you were asked, do you think you could recite the Ten Commandments?"

—— Yes, but not the exact words.
—— Yes, the exact words.
—— I'm not sure that I would remember all ten.

Table 50 shows how church members rate their own knowledge of the Ten Commandments. The data show that despite all the efforts in catechetical classes, very few Protestants think they could recite the exact words of the Ten Commandments—from a low of 1 percent of the Congregationalists to a high of 27 percent of the Missouri Synod Lutherans. Overall, only 9 percent of the Protestants think they would remember the exact words, while a third (34%) of the Roman Catholics think they could do so. Combined with some interesting irregularities in the Protestant data, this contrast between Protestants and Catholics suggests that, like the importance placed on ritual practices for gaining salvation (see Chapter 2) knowledge of the exact words of the Ten Commandments is related to the degree to which a denomination has a "high church" or liturgical tradition. Thus, among the most liberal Protestant bodies the Episcopalians are more likely to say they know the Ten Commandments than are the less liturgical Congregationalists, Methodists, or Disciples of Christ. Similarly, the Lutheran groups are more likely to say they know the commandments than are the less liturgical Presbyterians, Baptists, and sect members. (These contrasts are shown by the boldface figures in the table.) These differences are undoubtedly due to the greater emphasis on catechetical instruction in the Roman Catholic, Lutheran, and Episcopalian traditions.

But if the lesson of the Ten Commandments has not been mastered in its exact wording, has it been mastered in substance? The data show that slightly more than half of the Protestants and three-quarters of the Catholic church members claim they could recite all ten even if incorrectly. Forty-four percent of the Congregationalists and 46 percent of the Methodists make this claim. The more conservative Protestant bodies—the Missouri Lutherans, Southern Baptists, and sect members—closely approximate the Roman Catholic figure of 74 percent.

Keeping in mind that these are church members' own reports of their knowledge, and not a *test* of that knowledge, these figures

Table 50

KNOWLEDGE OF TEN COMMANDMENTS (Church-Member Sample)

"If you were asked, do you think you could recite the Ten Commandments?"

	Congre-gational	Metho-dist	Episco-palian	Disciples of Christ	Presby-terian	American Baptist	American Lutheran	Missouri Lutheran	Southern Baptist	Sects	TOTAL Protestant	Roman Catholic
Number:	(151)	(415)	(416)	(50)	(495)	(208)	(141)	(116)	(79)	(255)	(2,326)	(545)
Percentage who answered:												
Yes, the exact words.	1	4	13	4	5	19	5	27	10	14	9	34
Yes, but not the exact words.	43	42	51	48	40	44	48	44	67	60	46	40
Total who think they know commandments	44%	46%	64%	52%	45%	61%	53%	71%	77%	74%	55%	74%

must be judged as the highest possible estimate of the degree to which the churches have succeeded in teaching the Ten Commandments. Yet, even these estimates show that only a bare majority of the Protestants think they can even remember the content of the Ten Commandments and a mere 9 percent say they could recite them exactly. Catholics reveal a considerably more knowledgeable picture. This should not be generalized, however. As we shall see shortly, when objective tests were made of church members' knowledge of teachings and traditions, Catholics were consistently much *less* informed than Protestants.

Aside from knowing the content of the Ten Commandments it is possible to ask something about the knowledge church members have of the historical and cultural tradition of this moral code. Specifically, do they know the Ten Commandments are part of the Judaic legacy to Christianity? Turning to Table 51 we can see the proportions of church members who know that Jews also "believe in the Ten Commandments." Interestingly, among Protestants in general this information was more commonly known (by 77%) than the substance of the commandments themselves. Among Roman Catholics fewer knew this (66%) than said they knew the commandments. There are no important differences among the Protestant bodies in the proportions knowing that the Jews too believe in the Ten Commandments—still, roughly a quarter of Christian church members do not know this.

This question on the Jews and the Ten Commandments was also included in the national study. The data in Table 52 show that members of the general American public are less likely to know that Jews and Christians share in the Ten Commandments than are Americans who belong to church congregations. The national data show that 62 percent of the Roman Catholics knew this, and 52 percent of the Protestants did so. Among Protestants, members of the more liberal churches are somewhat more likely to know Jews believe in the Ten Commandments than are the members of the more conservative bodies. It is questionable, however, whether this fact is taught primarily by religious institutions or is primarily inculcated via the secular culture. The continuing efforts to mitigate anti-Semitism by stressing the

Table 51

KNOWLEDGE OF JEWISH BELIEF IN THE TEN COMMANDMENTS (Church-Member Sample)

	Congre-gational	Metho-dist	Episco-palian	Disciples of Christ	Presby-terian	American Lutheran	American Baptist	Missouri Lutheran	Southern Baptist	Sects	TOTAL Protestant	Roman Catholic
Number:	(151)	(415)	(416)	(50)	(495)	(208)	(141)	(116)	(79)	(255)	(2,326)	(545)
"Do Jews believe in the Ten Commandments?" Percentage who answered:												
Yes.	77	79	77	82	81	68	78	75	72	70	77	66
No.	11	4	6	8	4	6	6	8	8	9	5	10
Don't know and no answer.	12	17	17	10	15	25	16	17	20	21	18	24

Table 52

KNOWLEDGE OF JEWISH BELIEF IN TEN COMMANDMENTS (National Sample)

	"Do Jews believe in the Ten Commandments?"			
	Yes	No	Don't know	
Unitarian (9)	67	0	33	100%
Congregational (44)	72	7	21	100%
United Presbyterian (76)	54	11	35	100%
Protestant Episcopal (57)	68	7	25	100%
Methodist (218)	51	8	41	100%
Presbyterian Church U.S. (40)	70	8	22	100%
The Christian Church (42)	46	10	44	100%
American Lutheran bodies	47	12	41	100%
Lutheran, Missouri Synod (46)	39	20	41	100%
Evangelical Reform (28)	50	21	29	100%
American Baptist (92)	47	10	43	100%
Southern Baptist (187)	51	6	43	100%
Other Baptist bodies (92)	48	11	41	100%
Sects (132)	52	10	38	100%
Total Protestant (1,209)	52	10	38	100%
Roman Catholic (507)	62	12	26	100%

commonality of Jews and Christians have primarily been aspects of secular rather than religious institutions, and these may have been the effective sources of this information on the Ten Commandments. Consequently this item seems of questionable validity for measuring religious knowledge.

KNOWLEDGE OF SCRIPTURE

That nineteenth-century champion of skepticism, Colonel Robert G. Ingersoll, once remarked, "Everybody talks about the Bible and nobody reads it; that is the reason it is so generally believed." [1] We have seen in Chapter 4 that Ingersoll was at least partly right: A majority of Protestant and an overwhelming number of Catholic church members rarely if ever read the Bible. Yet this does not necessarily mean they are ignorant of its contents. Religious institutions are constantly teaching what the Bible says, and likely many persons know much from the Bible that they have never personally read. Still, what Ingersoll had in mind was that there is much in the Bible that is rarely mentioned by the churches and which would, if they knew about it, trouble persons who proclaim literal belief in the Bible.

A battery of items included in the questionnaire presented respondents with a series of quotations. For each, church members were asked to judge whether or not it appeared in the Bible. These questions will allow us both to estimate the extent to which church members know their scripture and to see whether they are especially ignorant of passages that the modern mind would find difficult to accept as literally true. Turning to the data shown in Table 53 we may adduce some answers to these questions. The quotations are presented in the order in which respondents showed the greatest scriptural ignorance.

The first quotation, "Thou shalt not suffer a witch to live," is scriptural (Exodus 22:18) and was probably well known in past centuries when the burning of witches was common. Today, such practices are regarded as horrors of a benighted and brutal age. Correspondingly, the knowledge that the practice of witch burning, and indeed belief in the existence of witches, is based on Holy Scripture is rare indeed. Only 11 percent of the Protestants and 3 percent of the Catholics correctly identified this quotation as from the Bible. Interestingly enough, almost a third of those who belong to small Protestant sects did recognize this quotation as biblical.

Of even greater importance is personal agreement with the

[1] As an indication of the changes in the American religious climate, Ingersoll's writings, filled with remarks like this, today retain their wit, but very little of their ability to shock. It was not always so: "If Bob Ingersoll isn't in hell, God is a liar and the Bible isn't worth the paper it is printed on" (Billy Sunday, reported in the *Courier*, Jacksonville, Ill., October 27, 1908).

statement. For each quotation, respondents were asked to "please indicate whether or not you agree with the statement. Please do this even if you think the statement is not from the Bible."

The majority of those who knew this statement was from the Bible agreed with it! Twenty-two percent of the sect members personally agreed that witches should be executed as did 7 percent of all Protestants and 2 percent of the Roman Catholics. Perhaps surprisingly, not all Christian church members have rejected the reality of witchcraft. But more interesting is the fact that knowledge of the biblical sources of this quotation is almost exclusively limited to those who accept its truth—those who reject the practice of burning witches are almost unanimously ignorant that the Bible clearly teaches this. These findings lend support to Ingersoll's charges.

The second quotation is not so potentially troubling, and a great many more church members know it to be in fact biblical: "Let your women keep silence in the churches: for it is not permitted unto them to speak." Forty-three percent of the Protestants and 24 percent of the Catholics answered correctly. Still, the majority of Christian church members did not know it to be biblical. Among Protestants, knowledge of this verse varied greatly among the denominations: while 30 percent of the Methodists, 32 percent of the Episcopalians, and 34 percent of the Congregationalists knew of it, 68 percent of the Southern Baptists, and 80 percent of the sect members did so. Many persons who knew this statement to be biblical nevertheless rejected its truth: only 11 percent of the Protestants and 20 percent of the Catholics personally agreed with the statement. Among Protestants, agreement was concentrated among the conservatives, 30 percent of the Southern Baptists and sect members agreed with the verse. Thus, perhaps contrary to what Ingersoll thought, many church members *are* able to reject the validity of statements they know to be biblical.

The third item in the table was contrived. A large number of church members were fooled by an invented quotation which copied the form of statements contained in the Sermon on the Mount, but clearly violated the spirit of this soaring moral teach-

Table 53

RECOGNITION OF BIBLE VERSES (Church-Member Sample)

"Now would you please read each of the following statements and . . . decide whether the statement is from the Bible or not."

	Congre-gational	Metho-dist	Episco-palian	Disciples of Christ	Presby-terian	American Lutheran	American Baptist	Missouri Lutheran	Southern Baptist	Sects	TOTAL Protestant	Roman Catholic
Number:	(151)	(415)	(416)	(50)	(495)	(208)	(141)	(116)	(79)	(255)	(2,326)	(545)
1. Thou shalt not suffer a witch to live.												
Percentage correct (Yes)	8	8	7	8	8	5	13	9	15	32	11	3
2. Let your women keep silence in the churches: for it is not permitted unto them to speak.												
Percentage correct (Yes)	34	30	32	58	40	36	49	55	68	80	43	24
3. Blessed are the strong: for they shall be the sword of God.												
Percentage correct (No)	72	73	66	78	74	67	78	60	80	83	72	59

4. For I the Lord thy God am a jealous God, visiting the iniquity of the fathers upon the children unto the third and fourth generation of them that hate me.											
Percentage correct (Yes)											
74	72	81	78	79	83	77	88	80	86	79	34

5. For it is easier for a camel to go through a needle's eye, than for a rich man to enter into the kingdom of God.											
Percentage correct (Yes)											
79	79	80	94	84	80	91	72	92	95	83	62

6. Blessed are the meek: for they shall inherit the earth.											
Percentage correct (Yes)											
97	96	96	96	97	95	98	97	95	98	96	87

ing. The content of "Blessed are the strong: for they shall be the sword of God," profoundly contradicts the moral vision embodied in such verses as "Blessed are the merciful: for they shall obtain mercy." Indeed, the content of this contrived quotation is akin to items used in the usual measures of authoritarianism, a far cry from the meekness, humility, and gentleness of the Sermon on the Mount.

Still, nearly 30 percent of the Protestants and more than 40 percent of the Roman Catholics failed to detect this quotation as spurious, and 25 percent of the Protestants and 32 percent of the Catholics personally agreed with its message.

Quotation four is from the twentieth chapter of Exodus where the Ten Commandments appear, and in many Christian catechisms this passage is to be memorized as an amplification of the First Commandment. Overall, 79 percent of the Protestants did in fact recognize that "For I the Lord thy God am a jealous God, visiting the iniquity of the fathers upon the children unto the third and fourth generation of them that hate me" is biblical. However, only a third of the Roman Catholics did so. Recall that Roman Catholics were much more likely than Protestants to say they *knew* the Ten Commandments and more likely than Protestants to claim to be able to recite them exactly. But this self-reporting must now be evaluated in light of the fact that more than twice as many Protestants as Catholics recognized the biblical origins of a statement commonly associated with (if not included in) the Ten Commandments. In addition, 43 percent of the Protestants and 19 percent of the Catholics thought this statement was true, that God does punish unto the third and fourth generations.

The fifth quotation is the famous biblical statement "For it is easier for a camel to go through a needle's eye, than for a rich man to enter into the kingdom of God," and it is no surprise that 83 percent of the Protestants recognized it as such. On the other hand, more than a third of the Catholics failed to identify this verse as biblical. While a vast majority of church members knew this statement was from the Bible, a majority did not personally agree with it: 47 percent of the Protestants and 39 percent of the Catholics did agree. Of even greater interest is that agreement to this statement sharply declined as the median income of denominations increased. Among the Congregationalists, for example, 64 percent of whom have incomes in excess of $10,000 a year, only 28 percent personally agreed that it is nearly impossible for the rich to enter heaven, while among the Southern Baptists, only 26 percent of whom earn above $10,000 a year, 85 percent agreed with the Bible. This suggests that church members can accommodate some uncomfortable scriptural teachings more proficiently than Colonel Ingersoll might have imagined, by the simple technique of denying the validity of some portions of the Bible. In Ingersoll's day the prevalent doctrine was literal acceptance of the Bible as absolutely true in its entirety. Today, many Christians regard Scripture as inspired, but not necessarily literally true. Thus, the dilemmas which Ingersoll proclaimed have largely evaporated.

The last item in the table was included merely to obtain the maximum possible measurement of scriptural literacy. Church members who failed to recognize that "Blessed are the meek: for they shall inherit the earth," was from the Bible can only be judged as extraordinarily ignorant. And, as might be expected, this knowledge is nearly universal—96 percent of the Protestants knew this Bible passage although fewer Catholics, 87 percent, did so. Given the easiness of the question, however, it seems quite meaningful that as many as 13 percent of the Catholics did not recognize it. Indeed, looking again at the table, it can be seen that Protestants were considerably more likely than Catholics to give the correct answer on every one of the questions. Furthermore, *every Protestant denomination surpassed the Catholics in the proportion with correct answers on every single question.*

The question arises as to how much of this superior Protestant knowledge of Scriptures simply reflects the fact that Catholics are much less likely to read the Bible than are Protestants (and that the Catholic Church places much less emphasis on scriptural knowledge among laymen), and how much of this difference can be attributed to a Protestant superiority on religious knowledge in general? Later in this chapter we shall examine items not based solely on scriptural knowledge in an effort to resolve this question.

To summarize these data on knowledge of the Bible, a Scriptural Knowledge Index was constructed by giving respondents one point for each correct answer on this set of questions. (The question on "Blessed are the meek . . ." was omitted because it was so well known that it was not useful for differentiating among respondents.) Thus, persons could score as low as zero by missing all of the questions or as high as five by answering them all correctly. The original index was collapsed into three groups for ease in presentation. The High group is composed of those who got at least four of the five questions correct. The Medium group gave three correct answers, and those scored as Low gave two or fewer correct answers.[2] Turning to Table 54 we may see how the denominations compare overall on this summary of their scriptural knowledge. As is immediately apparent, the differences are very great. While 40 percent of the Protestants scored high on the index, only 13 percent of the Catholics did so; and while only 27 percent of the Protestants received low scores, nearly two-thirds, 62 percent, of the Catholics scored low. Among the Protestants, the Methodists scored lowest with only 27 percent in the high category, while 67 percent of the Southern Baptists and 79 percent of the sect members scored high.

In summary, knowledge of the Scriptures is relatively low among the liberal and moderate Protestant groups, and very low among Roman Catholics, but very high in the most conservative Protestant bodies.

THE OLD TESTAMENT PROPHETS

In another effort to assess church members' knowledge of their religious culture, respondents were asked to identify the Old Testament prophets included in the following list of names:

[2] Persons who failed to answer any item were eliminated from the index.

Table 54

DISTRIBUTIONS ON SCRIPTURAL KNOWLEDGE INDEX (Church-Member Sample)

	Congre-gational	Metho-dist	Episco-palian	Disciples of Christ	Presby-terian	American Lutheran	American Baptist	Missouri Lutheran	Southern Baptist	Sects	TOTAL Protestant	Roman Catholic
Number:	(117)	(338)	(327)	(40)	(388)	(158)	(108)	(87)	(63)	(206)	(1,836)	(379)
Identification of Bible Quotations												
High 4,5	28%	27%	30%	55%	39%	31%	48%	43%	67%	79%	40%	13%
Medium 3	42	41	40	25	35	35	35	26	16	16	33	25
Low 0–2	30	32	30	20	26	34	17	31	17	5	27	62

Elijah
Deuteronomy
Jeremiah
Paul
Leviticus
Ezekiel

The majority of Protestants did well on this question with 79 percent, 78 percent, and 73 percent respectively correctly identifying Elijah, Jeremiah, and Ezekiel as the prophets included in the list. Catholics did not do as well, 57 percent, 59 percent, and 50 percent respectively were correct. Both Protestants (95%) and Catholics (91%) did best in excluding Paul as an Old Testament prophet, while Protestants were most likely to err in thinking Deuteronomy (30%) was the name of a prophet, and Catholics did worst on recognizing Ezekiel as a prophet, since half of them failed to choose him from the list.

To get some overall estimate of how respondents did on this question, it was scored as if it were a simple quiz. Thus, church members received one point for each correct answer, that is, for properly picking or omitting each name on the list. Possible scores range from a perfect six down to zero for missing on all six. The results for each denomination are shown in Table 55. Forty-three percent of the Protestants got all six correct, while 22 percent of the Catholics got this high a score; 36 percent of the Protestants got medium scores of four or five correct, while 40 percent of the Catholics did so; and 21 percent of the Protestants obtained low scores of zero through three, and 38 percent of the Catholics secured similar scores. Indeed, in all Protestant denominations a larger proportion of the members made high scores than did Roman Catholics. Still, variation among the Protestants was quite substantial. While 35 percent of the Congregationalists and 36 percent of the Episcopalians earned high scores, 58 percent of the Southern Baptists and 75 percent of the sect members did so.

THE RELIGIOUS KNOWLEDGE INDEX

To construct a general measure of religious knowledge the scores achieved on knowledge of scriptural quotations and of Old

Table 55

IDENTIFICATION OF OLD TESTAMENT PROPHETS (Church-Member Sample)

	Congre-gational	Metho-dist	Episco-palian	Disciples of Christ	Presby-terian	American Lutheran	American Baptist	Missouri Lutheran	Southern Baptist	Sects	TOTAL Protestant	Roman Catholic
Number:	(151)	(415)	(416)	(50)	(495)	(208)	(141)	(116)	(79)	(255)	(2,326)	(545)
Identification of Old Testament prophets												
High 6	35%	38%	36%	56%	44%	29%	47%	36%	58%	75%	43%	22%
Medium 4,5	37	34	42	38	35	46	38	38	28	21	36	40
Low 0-3	28	28	22	6	21	25	15	26	14	4	21	38

Testament prophets were combined.[3] The validity of the index which resulted was checked by its powerful predictions of knowledge of the Jewish origins of the Ten Commandments and self-estimates of the ability to recite the Ten Commandments.

Table 56 shows the distribution of members of each denomination on the Religious Knowledge Index. Overall, Protestants are much more likely to score high on religious knowledge than are Roman Catholics. Twenty-seven percent of the Protestants scored high while only 5 percent of the Catholics did so. Furthermore, more than half (52%) of the Protestants scored medium or high, while only 21 percent of the Catholics did this well. In contrast, more than half of the Catholics (54%) scored at the lowest point on the index while 26 percent of the Protestants knew this little about their faith. Every Protestant body outscored the Catholics.

Among Protestants, however, the contrasts are extensive. While only 16 percent of the Methodists, and 17 percent of the Episcopalians and Congregationalists scored high, 51 percent of the Southern Baptists and 69 percent of those in sects did so. But perhaps the surprise of the table is that while the extreme left and extreme right Protestant bodies differ greatly in the way we have come to expect on other measures of religious commitment, religious knowledge does not systematically rise through the middle of the table. The Lutherans, through their relatively poor performances, cause a sag in the middle. The American Lutheran bodies fall below the performances of Presbyterians and the American Baptists—indeed, American Lutherans have the smallest proportion of high scorers of any Protestant body. Similarly, the Missouri Lutherans, who show extraordinarily large propor-

[3] The scoring was: Identification of Bible Quotations:
High = 2
Medium = 1
Low = 0
Identification of Old Testament Prophets:
High = 2
Medium = 1
Low = 0

Table 56
RELIGIOUS KNOWLEDGE (Church-Member Sample)

	Congregational	Methodist	Episcopalian	Disciples of Christ	Presbyterian	American Lutheran	American Baptist	Missouri Lutheran	Southern Baptist	Sects	TOTAL Protestant	Roman Catholic
Number:	(151)	(415)	(416)	(50)	(495)	(208)	(141)	(116)	(79)	(255)	(2,326)	(545)
Religious Knowledge Index												
High	17%	16%	17%	40%	26%	15%	30%	23%	51%	69%	27%	5%
Medium	23	24	26	28	29	22	32	24	21	18	25	16
Medium Low	31	29	26	15	20	25	16	24	10	7	22	25
Low	29	31	31	17	25	38	22	29	18	5	26	54

tions of highly committed persons on other dimensions of involvement, fall way down on religious knowledge. Instead of showing
proportions similar to the Southern Baptists (51%), whose pattern they approach on other kinds of commitment, 23 percent of
the Missouri Lutherans scored high on religious knowledge.

A possible explanation for this sudden departure of the Lutherans from the customary left-right pattern of commitment may be
that, like the Catholics, they place great reliance on a catechetical
form of religious training. Confirmation class instruction in Lu-
theranism has mostly consisted of the rote learning of Luther's
catechism, at least until very recently. These findings, combined
with those for Catholics, who also use this kind of rote instruction, suggest that this traditional method may be rather ineffec-
tive. In contrast to the success of these bodies in obtaining commitment to other religious modes, their religious instruction seems
a definite failure.

NATIONAL RELIGIOUS KNOWLEDGE

Only the single question on whether Jews accept the Ten Commandments was included as a measure of religious knowledge in
our national survey. However, some information on the state of
general public religious knowledge is available from a 1954 nationwide Gallup Poll.[4] There seem two good reasons for presenting these Gallup findings in this chapter. First of all, we have
commented in passing that to some extent our picture of Catholic
religious knowledge might be slightly biased by the nature of our
items. Since Catholics make so little personal use of the Bible,
questions about biblical quotations may more accurately reflect
the state of knowledge among Protestants than among Catholics
(although they seem perfectly suitable for analytic purposes even
if they are descriptively misleading). Similarly, the identification
of Old Testament prophets (and the identification of apostles and
books of the Bible as *not* being Old Testament prophets) may

[4] Study No. 539-K. Data and codes were supplied by the International Data
Library and Reference Service of the Survey Research Center, University of
California, Berkeley.

give Protestants an advantage. Thus, the Gallup data provide an occasion to examine Catholic knowledge on a wider range of questions.

Secondly, the Gallup data provide a descriptive opportunity for examining the religious knowledgeability of the public at large, not just church members.

Turning to the data in Table 57, a number of generalizations are possible:

1. The public on the whole is amazingly ignorant of what seem to be unbelievably obvious questions. For example, 79 percent of

Table 57
RELIGIOUS KNOWLEDGE IN THE AMERICAN POPULATION (Gallup, 1954)

	Protestants (1,052)	Catholics (328)	Jews (41)
What is the first book of the Bible?			
Percentage correct:	59	19	34
Where was Jesus born?			
Percentage correct:	66	61	44
Who delivered the Sermon on the Mount?			
Percentage correct:	36	28	25
Who was the mother of Jesus?			
Percentage correct:	95	94	91
Will you name the founder of one religion besides Christianity?			
Percentage who could:	32	25	39 *
What is the Holy Trinity?			
Percentage correct:	33	60	37
Will you name two major prophets mentioned in the Old Testament of the Bible?			
Percentage who could name at least one:	21	14	25
One person wrote most of the books in the New Testament. Can you name that person?			
Percentage correct:	22	6	17
What country ruled Jerusalem during the time of Jesus?			
Percentage correct:	35	34	59

* Jews did not receive credit for founders of Judaism.

the Protestants and 86 percent of the Catholics could not name a *single* Old Testament prophet! More than two-thirds of American Christians do not know who preached the Sermon on the Mount! More than a third did not know where Jesus was born!

2. Catholics do much better on questions which are less dependent upon the Bible, but except for knowledge that the Holy Trinity is made up of Father, Son, and Holy Ghost, they are still generally less knowledgeable than are Protestants.

3. Jews are surprisingly well informed on Christian matters. They were nearly as likely as Catholics to know who preached the Sermon on the Mount, they exceeded Protestants in identifying the Holy Trinity, and they surpassed Catholics in knowing who wrote most of the books of the *New* Testament. They surpassed Catholics in identifying the first book of the Bible. (Only 19% of America's Catholics could answer "Genesis.") On other matters directly pertaining to Judaism, such as Old Testament prophets, they were the highest of the three major religious groups.

These data present an ironic picture of American religion. Virtually everyone has a denomination, but few know even trivial facts about their faith.

Chapter 8

CHURCHES AS MORAL COMMUNITIES

*A religion is a unified system of beliefs and practices
relative to sacred things, that is to say, things set
apart and forbidden—beliefs and practices which unite
into one single moral community called a Church, all
those who adhere to them.*
Emile Durkheim

In this chapter we shall shift our attention
from individual criteria of religious commitment to examine the
character of the relationships which church members establish
with their churches. The church can be a central institution in a
person's life absorbing much of his energy and providing a primary source of his friendships and social contacts. Or, a person's
attachments to the church may be merely nominal counting little
in the total context of his life. Religious thinkers through the ages
have affirmed the ideal that a church should be "a community of
believers," as exemplified by the Christian churches of the first
and second centuries. In such an ideal community members are
united by strong and intimate interpersonal bonds. Groups in
which such close social relations exist constitute what social scientists call a "primary group," because of the importance for the
individual of his ties to such groups. Charles H. Cooley, who first
introduced the term "primary group" in his 1909 book, *Social
Organization,* spoke of the "wholeness" that characterizes such
groups.[1] "Perhaps the simplest way of describing this wholeness is
by saying that it is a 'we'; it involves the sort of sympathy and
mutual identification for which 'we' is the natural expression." [2]

[1] New York: Charles Scribner's Sons.
[2] *Ibid.,* p. 23.

A criterion of the ideal church, then, is that it function as a primary group. In turn, a criterion for the ideal church member is that he be related to his church by bonds of friendship and affection. Gerhard Lenski has identified this kind of attachment of church members to their churches as *communal involvement*.[3]

But it has long been recognized that these ideals are frequently, and perhaps typically, not fulfilled either by churches or by church members in actual practice. Indeed, the fact that churches have drifted away from this "authentic" state has been a central concern of religious reformers throughout the centuries. Perhaps the majority of dissident religious movements have aimed to establish a religious group that would approach the ideal of community.

What has come to be called "church-sect theory" represents an effort by social scientists to describe and account for this friction between the ideal and the actual. Briefly, this body of theory postulates that social forces acting upon religious organizations are such that they are almost invariably transformed from moral communities (sects) into more formal and less intimate organizations (churches). We have elsewhere questioned the utility of limiting the classification of religious bodies to sects and churches.[4] However, it remains that religious bodies do differ in these ways, and that individual members differ greatly in the extent to which they are tied to their churches by bonds of friendship.

It must be recognized that the ideal of communal involvement applies at two levels of analysis. On the one hand we may speak of the extent to which a church constitutes a primary group. We may also speak of the extent to which the church serves as a pri-

[3] Gerhard Lenski, *The Religious Factor* (Garden City, N.Y.: Doubleday, 1961), especially pp. 21–22.

[4] Charles Y. Glock and Rodney Stark, *Religion and Society in Tension* (Chicago: Rand McNally, 1965), ch. 13. See also the theoretical discussion in Stephen Steinberg, "Reform Judaism: The Origin and Evolution of a 'Church Movement,'" *Journal for the Scientific Study of Religion*, V, No. 1 (1965), pp. 117–129, and the extremely important paper by Benton Johnson, "On Church and Sect," *American Sociological Review*, XXVIII, No. 4 (1963), pp. 539–549.

mary group for any individual member, whether or not it does so for most of its members.

At the level of the church we have in mind a continuum. At one pole is a church whose membership might be called a religious audience, at the other is a church whose membership constitutes a religious community. A church's membership represents a religious audience when it is composed of persons who gather periodically to participate in worship, but no network of interpersonal relations binds them together. Thus, they resemble other audiences, such as those that gather in movie theaters or in sports stadia. The polar type at the other end of this continuum is characterized by bonds of interpersonal relationships that unite the participants. This is the religious community in which participants know one another and share much more than the transitory proximity of being in an audience.

Whether or not a church tends to be a religious audience or a religious community it is possible for individual members to participate either as part of an audience or as members of a community. Although most members in a church may lack all interpersonal ties to other members, a minority could still maintain primary relations within the congregation. Conversely, although the majority may constitute a primary group, a minority could simply remain unrelated strangers. In subsequent volumes we shall examine the importance of communal involvement for other aspects of human behavior. For the present, our concern is to measure and describe the extent to which modern churches approach or fall short of this ideal.

We shall begin by examining the extent of friendship among church members. Respondents were asked:

> Of your five closest friends, how many are members of your congregation or parish?

Table 58 shows the extent to which contemporary Christian denominations are united by friendship. The overwhelming majority of Christians report that most of their five best friends are not members of their church congregation. While 29 percent of the Protestants said at least three are members of their congrega-

Table 58

CONGREGATIONAL FRIENDSHIP (Church-Member Sample)

"Of five best friends, how many belong to your congregation?"

	Congregational	Methodist	Episcopalian	Disciples of Christ	Presbyterian	American Lutheran	American Baptist	Missouri Lutheran	Southern Baptist	Sects	TOTAL Protestant	Roman Catholic
Number:	(151)	(415)	(416)	(50)	(495)	(208)	(141)	(116)	(79)	(255)	(2,326)	(545)
Percentage who answered:												
Three to five.	18	24	20	42	23	20	40	25	49	67	29	36
Two.	11	17	19	10	19	14	13	15	11	13	16	14
One.	22	16	21	12	18	15	12	19	14	7	16	14
None.	49	43	39	36	39	50	31	40	23	9	36	34
No answer.	0	0	1	0	1	1	4	1	3	4	3	2

tion, 36 percent of the Catholics said this. Furthermore, 36 percent of the Protestants and 34 percent of the Catholics reported that none of their five best friends were members of their congregation. Roughly speaking the overall Christian picture is one of thirds: a third have most of their friends in their congregation, a third have some friends, and a third have none.

But various Protestant bodies greatly depart from this general pattern. The Congregationalists, Methodists, Episcopalians, Presbyterians, and Lutherans have far less than a third of their members who have most of their friends in their church, and greatly exceed a third in the number with no friends. Indeed, 50 percent of the American Lutherans and 49 percent of the Congregationalists said *none* of their best friends belonged to their congregation. At the other extreme, 67 percent of the sect members and 49 percent of the Southern Baptists reported that most of their best friends were in their congregation. Indeed, 30 percent of the sect members and 20 percent of the Southern Baptists said that *all* of their five best friends were in their congregation!

Clearly American Christians differ greatly in the extent to which they are tied to their church congregations by bonds of friendship. But just as clearly the denominations differ greatly in the proportions of their members who are so tied. Examining the various denominations it is obvious that some resemble religious audiences while others come closer to the ideal of being religious communities. It is not possible to say absolutely just what proportion of a congregation ought to have how many friends from the congregation in order for the group to be called a true community or a primary group. Obviously it is not necessary that all be friends of all. For the sake of comparison, we shall adopt several relatively arbitrary but reasonable standards. If we can consider a person to be imbedded in a religious community if at least two of his five best friends are members of his church, then it seems clear that the small Protestant sect groups come rather close to the ideal of being religious communities—80 percent of their members restrict their friendship to fellow congregants to this extent. Among the major denominations the Southern Baptists are closest to this ideal with 60 percent of their members having at least two of their five best friends in their congregations. The Disciples of Christ, American Baptists, and Roman Catholics manage a bare majority of members who meet this standard of communal involvement. The least communally involved denomination is the Congregational Church with only 29 percent meeting our criterion of involvement. Thus, Christian churches range from religious audiences to religious communities and within all denominations the communal involvement of individual members varies greatly.

We have thus far examined the extent to which persons are bound to their churches by ties of friendship and the extent to which they limit their friendship to their fellow congregants. We shall now examine a somewhat more general measure of communal involvement: the extent to which persons limit their organizational participation to the church. In Chapter 4 we saw that church members vary greatly in the number of church activities and organizations in which they take part. While the sheer amount of organizational participation a person gives to his church is an important measure of his commitment, this can be substantially qualified by what portion of his total organizational participation is in the church. For example, one person may only take part in two church activities, while another takes part in four. But if the first person has no other organizational involvements, while the person with four church activities is also active in ten secular organizations it follows that the first person is much more organizationally immersed in church than is the second. On the one hand, the church is the only outlet for the organizational activity of some persons, while for others the church is only one of many such outlets. This variety of communal involvement cannot be judged solely on the basis of the extent of organizational participation in the church. Thus, we must examine participation in both church and secular organizations.

All respondents were asked to complete the following battery of items on their participation in secular organizations.

> Now we would like to know something about the organizations and clubs you belong to. Below are listed various kinds

of organizations. In the blank in front of each kind of organization, write in the number of organizations like this to which you belong. If none, mark 0.

_____ FRATERNAL GROUPS, such as Elks, Eagles, Masons, Knights of Columbus, Eastern Star, and women's auxiliaries to groups like this, etc.

_____ SERVICE CLUBS, such as Lions, Rotary, Zonta, Jr. Chamber of Commerce, etc.

_____ VETERANS GROUPS, such as the American Legion, VFW, Amvets, etc.

_____ POLITICAL GROUPS, such as Democratic or Republican clubs, and political action groups such as voter's leagues, NAACP, etc.

_____ LABOR UNIONS, such as International Typographical Union, Teamsters, etc.

_____ SPORTS GROUPS, such as bowling teams, bridge clubs, or sports sponsoring groups such as Downtown Quarterbacks, etc.

_____ YOUTH GROUPS, such as Boy Scouts, Girl Scouts, 4-H, etc.

_____ SCHOOL SERVICE GROUPS, such as PTA, or alumni associations, etc.

_____ HOBBY OR GARDEN CLUBS, such as stamp or coin clubs, flower clubs, pet clubs, etc.

_____ SCHOOL FRATERNITIES OR SORORITIES, such as Sigma Chi, Delta Gamma, etc.

_____ NATIONALITY GROUPS, such as Sons of Norway, Hibernian Society, etc.

_____ FARM ORGANIZATIONS, such as Farmer's Union, Farm Bureau, Grange, etc.

_____ LITERARY, ART, DISCUSSION, OR STUDY CLUBS, such as book review clubs, theater groups, painting groups, etc.

_____ PROFESSIONAL OR ACADEMIC SOCIETIES, such as the American Dental Association, Phi Beta Kappa, etc.

_____ OTHER ORGANIZATIONS NOT LISTED ABOVE (please write in) _____

_____

_____

For each respondent the total number of organizations he reported belonging to in this battery was computed. The figures were quite amazing. Surveys of a nationwide sample of American adults typically find that about 50 percent say they belong to no voluntary organizations.[5] In our sample of church members only 16 percent said they belonged to no such groups. Similarly, while only about 12 percent of Americans in general report belonging to three or more such organizations, 49 percent of these church members had this number of organizational affiliations. Clearly, church members are active "joiners" in contrast with the general public. Of course, at least for Protestants, membership in a church congregation is itself an act of joining and thus our respondents are preselected for their likelihood to belong to organizations. In addition, of course, as remarked in Chapter 4, church members are likely to be middle and upper class persons and past studies have shown that organizational participation of all kinds is predominately a middle and upper class activity.

Membership in voluntary organizations is common in all Christian denominations, but nevertheless the proportion of joiners differs considerably among them. Thus, 91 percent of the Congregationalists and 90 percent of the Methodists belonged to one or more voluntary organization, while 75 percent of the Southern Baptists and 70 percent of the sect members did so. Similarly, while 56 percent of the Congregationalists belonged to four or more organizations, only 15 percent of the Southern Baptists and 17 percent of the sect members belonged to this many.

[5] For a summary see: Bernard Lazerwitz, "Membership in Voluntary Associations and Frequency of Church Attendance," *Journal for the Scientific Study of Religion*, II, No. 1 (1962), pp. 74–84.

Our reason for computing the number of voluntary organizations to which individuals belong is to use it as a measure of the extent of their participation in secular activities. Of course it could be the case that persons belong to many secular organizations but are not active in them, while they are active in their religious organizations. However, the number of organizations to which a person belongs is a powerful predictor of his likelihood to spend time on non-church activities. Among Protestants 90 percent of those with seven or more organizational memberships report they attend a non-church meeting or other activity at least once a week, while only 2 percent of those who reported no organizational membership did so. Among Catholics the same comparison was 95 percent versus 4 percent. Thus membership is quite likely to engender participation in secular organizational affairs.

We may now combine these data with those reported in Chapter 4 on participation in church organizations to construct a measure of Communal Involvement. To produce this measure we relied upon a quite simple procedure. For each respondent we computed the percentage of all his organizational memberships (both secular and religious) which were religious.[6] Thus persons who belonged to one or more organizations, none of which were religious were scored as 0 percent on the Index of Communal Involvement. Similarly, persons could score as high as 100 percent if all of their memberships were in religious organizations.

Table 59 shows that church members differ greatly in the proportions of their total memberships which are religious. While 50 percent of the Episcopalians and 47 percent of the Congregationalists include no church groups in their organizational life, only 18 percent of the Southern Baptists and 22 percent of the sect members hold exclusively secular memberships. On the other hand, only 7 percent of the Congregationalists and 10 percent of the Episcopalians reported that 60 percent or more of their organizations were religious, while 43 percent of the Southern Baptists and 41 percent of the sect members did so. Indeed, 16 percent of

[6] Two hundred and thirty-six persons who belonged to no organizations, either secular or religious, were excluded from the data.

Table 59

COMMUNAL INVOLVEMENT (Church-Member Sample)

Proportion of total number of organizational memberships which are religious:

	Congre-gational	Metho-dist	Episco-palian	Disciples of Christ	Presby-terian	American Lutheran	American Baptist	Missouri Lutheran	Southern Baptist	Sects	TOTAL Protestant	Roman Catholic
Number:	(148)	(396)	(387)	(48)	(468)	(188)	(135)	(103)	(70)	(227)	(2,170)	(460)
Percentage who answered:												
60% or more.	7	14	10	31	17	21	22	27	43	41	19	9
40% to 59%.	12	18	9	29	19	20	23	17	62	24	18	10
10% to 39%.	34	29	31	19	31	27	29	25	13	13	27	24
0%*	47	39	50	21	33	32	26	31	18	22	36	57

* No respondent scored between 1% and 9%.

the Southern Baptists, 17 percent of the Missouri Lutherans, and 22 percent of the sect members completely limited their organizational participation to church groups. Overall, 19 percent of the Protestants find 60 percent or more of their organizational outlets in religion, while 9 percent of the Catholics do so.

Thus, whether it is measured in terms of bonds of friendship or in terms of the extent to which persons concentrate their organizational activities within the church, communal involvement produces marked differences among the Christian bodies. The more liberal denominations such as the Congregationalists, Methodists, and Episcopalians tend to constitute religious audiences. Their members are typically not bound to their religious congregation by personal friendships. Furthermore, in these more liberal bodies not only are members less likely to take part in church activities, but their church activities make up a relatively small proportion of their organizational outlets. In the most conservative bodies, however, such as the Southern Baptists and the various sects, the churches tend to function as primary groups composed of persons who restrict their friendships and their organizational activities to their congregations.

Emile Durkheim's conception of a church as a moral community is inapplicable to many contemporary Christian denominations. Today, to speak of churches as communities is also to speak of theologically conservative churches.

Chapter 9

PATTERNS OF FAITH

$$r = \frac{\Sigma(X - \bar{X})(Y - \bar{Y})}{\sqrt{[\Sigma(X - \bar{X})^2][\Sigma(Y - \bar{Y})^2]}}$$

Karl Pearson

The preceding chapters have been devoted to a series of measures of different aspects of religious commitment. Although we began with four general dimensions of commitment—belief, practice, knowledge, and experience—some additional sub-dimensions were added as we went along. Chart 1 summarizes the various measures that have been developed. Our basic set consists of five primary indices, but we shall also give some attention to four secondary measures.

Having developed all these measures of religious commitment we now come to the point where we must ask: Are all these really necessary? The initial parcelling out of religious commitment into these five primary and four secondary aspects was done on purely analytic grounds. This was, in the main, a logical and theoretical enterprise. But simply to postulate the logical possibility of these varieties of religious involvement in no way establishes the fact that the world in its complexity honors these logical possibilities. The fact is that while religious commitment *could* occur in these distinct modes, it may not. It is quite possible that in reality any pair or even all are so highly correlated with one another that they may not be empirically distinct. That is, religiousness of one kind may always occur in connection with another kind and never occur without it. If this should prove to be the case, then while we could still speak of several kinds of religiousness on analytic grounds, there would be little reason to do so for empirically they would have to be regarded as one and the same.

Chart 1

MEASURES OF RELIGIOUS COMMITMENT

General dimensions of religious commitment	Primary measures	Secondary measures
1. Belief	Orthodoxy Index	Particularism Index Ethicalism Index
2. Practice	Ritual Involvement Index Devotionalism Index	
3. Experience	Religious Experience Index	
4. Knowledge	Religious Knowledge Index	
	Relational Indices *	Communal Involvement Index Proportion of 5 best friends who belong to respondent's congregation

* Not part of the basic set of dimensions, these refer to the character of the relationships members form with their churches.

In this chapter we shall examine the empirical connections among our measures of religious commitment to determine the extent to which commitment is actually a unified or differentiated phenomenon.

First, however, it seems reasonable to explain why we chose to approach the problem in this way. It would seem equally appropriate to have begun with a unitary conception of religious commitment and then to see if it were possible empirically to detect the presence of multidimensionality within the data.

We had several reasons for beginning by postulating dimensionality and then testing the extent to which the dimensions were empirically independent. First of all, unless one has some understanding of the varieties of religious commitment which are logically possible, there is no basis for selecting the items originally to make up a general measure of commitment. For this reason, if one begins by assuming unidimensionality and later tests the data for multidimensionality there is no way to know that data on each possible dimension were included. Thus, for example, one might only have data on religious beliefs and ritual practice and the possibility that devotionalism, religious experiences, and religious knowledge might be other and somewhat different modes of commitment could never be discovered. If no measurement were made of these possible dimensions, no statistical technique could ever reveal them as a basis for treating religious commitment multidimensionally. Thus, in order to determine empirically whether or not religious commitment is unidimensional one must select appropriate data to make multidimensionality possible.

The second reason for beginning with such a broad conception of religious commitment was discussed in detail in Chapter 1. This has to do with credibility. We do not merely wish to discuss religious commitment as we define it, rather we are concerned with obtaining widespread initial agreement that commitment in *our* sense is a close approximation of what is *generally* meant by this term. Because we wish to make assertions about what is conventionally regarded as religious commitment, it was necessary to come to terms with conventional definitions. To the degree that we revise conventional conceptions of religious commitment in this chapter it will be in response to empirical findings, not preconceptions about what religiousness "really" is.

We may now turn to these empirical findings. In order to determine the question of how our postulated distinctions in religious involvement fit with contemporary reality the correlation coefficients among all of the indices constructed to measure these dimensions were computed.[1] The findings for Protestants appear in Table 60 and for Roman Catholics in Table 61. The implications of these data are rather complex, therefore the discussion is organized under a series of numbered points.

1. Overall, the intercorrelations are lower among Roman Catholics than among Protestants. The average of all correlations was $+.272$ for Protestants and $+.2$ for Catholics. Consequently, the distinctions among kinds of commitment are possibly more fully warranted among Catholics than among Protestants.

[1] Product moment correlations were generated by Alan B. Wilson's SA80 program.

Table 60

INTERCORRELATIONS AMONG THE DIMENSIONS OF RELIGIOUS COMMITMENT (Church-Member Sample)

Protestants

| | Chapter 3 | | | Chapter 4 | Chapter 5 | Chapter 6 | Chapter 7 | Chapter 8 | |
	Orthodoxy	Particularism	Ethicalism	Ritual	Devotional	Experience	Knowledge	Communal	Friendship
Orthodoxy	X	.555	−.020	.458	.506	.570	.306	.343	.337
Particularism		X	.080	.369	.315	.432	.156	.282	.311
Ethicalism			X	−.033	.060	.012	−.068	−.045	.023
Ritual				X	.360	.366	.356	.384	.355
Devotional					X	.467	.267	.237	.295
Experience						X	.276	.295	.321
Knowledge							X	.251	.249
Communal								X	.356
Friendship									X

Statistical significance for the above correlations may be assessed from the following computations for student's t (two tailed):

r equal to or greater than:	significant at:
.063	.001
.052	.01
.041	.05
.034	.10

Table 61

INTERCORRELATION AMONG THE DIMENSIONS OF RELIGIOUS COMMITMENT (Church-Member Sample)

Roman Catholics

	Chapter 3			Chapter 4	Chapter 5	Chapter 6	Chapter 7	Chapter 8	
	Orthodoxy	Particularism	Ethicalism	Ritual	Devotional	Experience	Knowledge	Communal	Friendship
Orthodoxy	X	.338	.111	.358	.501	.387	.133	.233	.114
Particularism		X	.311	.171	.288	.306	—.005	.152	.242
Ethicalism			X	.101	.169	.176	.059	.087	.110
Ritual				X	.365	.221	.162	.306	.114
Devotionalism					X	.424	.106	.250	.133
Experience						X	.045	.074	.133
Knowledge							X	.239	.052
Communal								X	.247
Friendship									X

r equal to or greater than:	significant at:
.14	.001
.11	.01
.09	.05
.07	.10

2. Of the various aspects of religious commitment, orthodoxy is the best single measure, although among Catholics devotionalism is equally good. Our criterion for calling orthodoxy "best" is that it has the highest average intercorrelation with the other indices among Protestants, while orthodoxy and devotionalism are about equal in their average intercorrelation among Catholics. What this means is that if one had to use only one of our various indices to measure religious commitment, orthodoxy would be the choice. It provides the best single estimate of how persons score on other aspects of commitment.[2] This confirms our assertion in Chapter 1 that theology is the core of commitment; it tells us more about the character of an individual's religious behavior than does any other aspect of commitment. However, it must be recognized that even though orthodoxy is the best overall measure, it is not exceptional when judged absolutely. Thus, the average intercorrelation of orthodoxy with other dimensions of commitment is only .382 among Protestants and .272 among Roman Catholics. These are relatively low correlations. This brings us to the more general question of whether religious commitment is empirically a unitary or multidimensional phenomenon.

3. The answer to this question requires some criterion of independence or unity. This is a vexing problem because statistical methods offer no hard-and-fast rule about how high a correlation should be in order for two indices to be considered measures of the same thing. For the lay reader it seems useful to state in

[2] This finding was also reported in a recent paper based on an independent operationalization of our analytic scheme. The authors developed their own questions to tap the various dimensions of religious commitment which we had earlier postulated. Their data, based on a small sample of college students, revealed patterns extremely similar to those in Tables 60 and 61. Orthodoxy was found to be the best single measure (actually they retained our original names and called their belief measure "Ideological commitment"). This lends considerable confidence to the stability of the independence among the dimensions of commitment; they are not an artifact of the items used, for similar patterns emerge from quite different items. See: Joseph E. Faulkner and Gordon F. De Jong, "Religiosity in 5-D: An Empirical Analysis," *Social Forces*, XLV, No. 2 (1966), pp. 246–254.

simple terms what a correlation means. A correlation coefficient, such as those which appear in Tables 60 and 61, expresses the extent to which a given index or measurement predicts a second index or measurement: for example, the extent to which knowing a man's score on orthodoxy allows a correct prediction of his score on devotionalism. A correlation is perfect when all scores on a given measurement can be predicted without error by the other measurement. Such a correlation is expressed as 1.0. It is extremely rare to find perfect correlations in social science; if nothing else, a few cases will have been miscoded or persons will have erred in marking an answer and thus produce a somewhat less than perfect correlation. A less than perfect correlation states the extent to which perfection is approached. One may think of two indices as represented by two circles. When a correlation is perfect the circles completely overlap one another. When there is absolutely no correlation between them they do not overlap at all. Correlations above 0 and below 1.0 reflect the extent to which they overlap. (A positive sign indicates one index predicts the presence of the other; a negative sign, the absence of the other.) The parts overlapping are the parts that measure the same thing. The parts that do not overlap measure different things and are the areas which are called independent.

The criterion we have adopted for calling two indices measures of the same thing is to require that more than half of the two circles overlap, that is, they have more in common than they are independent of one another. Conversely, if less than half of the circles overlap they are more measures of different things than they are measures of the same thing. Using this criterion, a correlation coefficient between two dimensions of religious commitment would have to slightly exceed .7 for the two to be called measures of the same thing (the extent to which the circles overlap is determined by squaring the correlation coefficient, thus with a correlation of .7 the two circles would be 49% overlapping). A glance at Tables 60 and 61 shows that no correlation between any two dimensions of commitment even approaches this standard. Indeed, the *highest* correlation among Protestants (between orthodoxy and religious experience) is only .570 (these two coincide only 32% of the time and vary independently 68% of the time). Among Catholics the highest correlation (between devotionalism and orthodoxy) is .501.

Clearly, these dimensions of religious commitment are much more independent of one another than they are measures of the same thing. What this means is that if we try to predict, for example, a man's score on ritual involvement from his score on orthodoxy we will not be very accurate.

The extent of independence found among the postulated dimensions of religious commitment is much more than sufficient to warrant our original analytic distinctions. Obviously, it was never expected that they would be unrelated, but merely that they might vary independently to an important extent, which in fact they do. Thus, these empirical findings require that the dimensions of religious commitment be treated as related, but distinct, manifestations of piety.[3]

4. If orthodoxy is the "best" single measure of religious commitment, by the same token ethicalism is the "poorest." Among Protestants, ethicalism is virtually unrelated to any other aspect of religiousness; indeed it seems to be weakly negatively related to orthodoxy, ritual, knowledge and communal involvement. These data force the conclusion that concern for man-to-man ethics is for all practical purposes not a part of general Protestant religious commitment. Those whose religiousness does take an ethical form are not especially apt to exhibit other kinds of religious commitment, while those who show considerable man-

[3] A further test of the independence of our dimensions of religious commitment was provided by a factor analysis carried out by Hiroko Rokumoto ("Factor Analysis of Religious Commitment," unpublished paper, Dept. of Sociology, University of California, Berkeley). Miss Rokumoto put all items used to construct the indices (as well as all validating items) into a factor analysis. The results were a striking confirmation of our analytic structure. The factors which emerged basically replicated our dimensions and indices. No item had its maximum loading on a factor on which an item from another dimension also had its maximum loading. While the proper use of factor analysis in social research is subject to considerable dispute, the findings do confirm that the postulated dimensions of religious commitment are empirically distinct.

to-God commitment seem to have little interest in the traditional ethical component of their faith.

Among Roman Catholics all of the correlations between ethicalism and other aspects of commitment are positive. This gives some support to the judgment that Catholicism has put more effective emphasis on the man-to-man ethical responsibilities of Christians than have Protestants.[4] Nevertheless, the correlations among Catholics are extremely weak and for the most part ethicalism—loving thy neighbor, and doing good for others—is not a typical component of Catholic religious commitment either.

5. In addition to these main findings, there are a great number of less important things to be read in Tables 60 and 61. Among these are: of primary measures the lowest correlation for both Protestants and Catholics is between particularism and knowledge which indicates a certain incompatibility between narrow religious partisanship and religious literacy; of the primary measures, knowledge is the "poorest" measure which suggests that knowledge about religion is not an especially religious phenomenon but is largely a part of knowledge and sophistication in general: informed persons know about religion whether or not they are otherwise religious; as would be expected the relational measures (communal involvement and having friends in one's congregation) are most strongly related to ritual involvement. The reader may wish to examine other combinations in the table to see how they are related.

To sum up the findings of this chapter, our initial assumption that religious commitment is a multidimensional phenomenon is verified empirically. The correlations among indices demonstrate that religious commitment is both logically and empirically a complex phenomenon.[5] Those who seek to understand man's religiousness must study it in its full complexity.

[4] The correlations were computed for various Protestant denominations separately and did not importantly differ from the general patterns reported in Table 60.

[5] Similar patterns of correlation were found among those aspects of religious commitment that could be measured in the national sample.

Chapter 10

THE SWITCHERS: CHANGES OF DENOMINATION

Take ye the sum of all the congregation of the children of Israel, after their families, by the house of their fathers, with the number of their names, every male by their polls.
Numbers 1:2 (A.V.)

It has always struck European observers as remarkable that Americans so commonly and easily change faiths. In the great American melting pot not only do ethnic lines soon become blurred, but the boundaries between faiths also seem to be easily crossed. We have become accustomed to reports of relatively high rates of conversion between Protestantism and Catholicism,[1] and in this culture of change we now recognize that there is considerable movement both into and out of Judaism.[2] Indeed, intermarriage across religious lines has become an important subject of social inquiry. But while there is considerable movement across the boundaries of the three main religious traditions, the overwhelming amount of church-switching that goes on in American society is within the Protestant community. Indeed, shifts from, for example, Methodism to Episcopalianism are so taken for granted in this country that they have been paid almost no heed. There are no published (and we know of no unpublished) statistics on the extent or patterns of intra-Protestant denominational switching.

In this chapter we shall attempt to remedy this lack of information. Is this vast amount of switching primarily random and idiosyncratic, or are some denominations gaining at the expense of others—are there important theological trends revealed by

[1] Both for rates and for a review of the literature see the excellent article by J. Milton Yinger, "Pluralism, Religion, and Secularism," *Journal for the Scientific Study of Religion*, VI, No. 1 (1967), pp. 17–28.

[2] See *ibid.*, and also Sidney Goldstein and Calvin Goldscheider, "Social and Demographic Aspects of Jewish Intermarriages," *Social Problems*, XIII, No. 4 (1966), pp. 386–399.

these shifts? A secondary concern with denominational switching stems from the fact that in subsequent volumes we want to control for the effect of childhood religious training. Thus we must be able to distinguish lifelong members of a given denomination from converts, and to know in what denomination a convert was raised.

We shall approach the question of denominational change first on the basis of our California church sample, and then examine national survey data to see how patterns may differ from region to region. We are only secondarily interested in shifts from Protestantism to Catholicism and vice versa. These have been studied elsewhere and tend largely to occur through marriage rather than to represent ideological switches.[3] Furthermore because of the way in which Protestants and Catholics were separately sampled we can only really take up this question in the national data. The small number of Jews in the national sample makes it impossible to draw any meaningful conclusions about switches to and from Judaism. Thus, we shall be primarily concerned with denominational changes within Protestantism.

To say that such changes among Protestants are common is an understatement. Nearly half (46%) of our Protestant respondents said that they had previously been members of a denomination other than the one to which they presently belonged. The crucial question raised by this fact is from whence to hence?

Table 62 gives the pattern of denominational turnover for our sample of church members. For several reasons these data somewhat underestimate the total amount of denomination switching, however they ought to be quite adequate to indicate trends.[4] A

[3] For a summary see: Sidney H. Croog and James E. Teele, "Religious Identity and Church Attendance of Sons of Religious Intermarriages," *American Sociological Review*, XXXII, No. 1 (1967), pp. 93–103.

[4] Because of a decision made when the original data were coded the table reports not the denomination in which respondents grew up, but instead their most recent previous denomination. However, since 76% of those who changed faiths did so only once this is the denomination in which they were raised. All but a handful of the remainder had changed only twice. In addition, the table omits persons who failed to specify what their earlier denominational affiliation was. It also masks the changes from one sect to another within the sect category.

Table 62

MOST RECENT FORMER DENOMINATION AND PRESENT DENOMINATION (Church-Member Sample; Protestants only)

Respondent's present denomination is:	Respondent's most recent former denomination was:									
Number:	Congregational (141)	Methodist (470)	Episcopalian (269)	Disciples of Christ (71)	Presbyterian (386)	American Lutheran [a] (212)	American Baptist [a] (148)	Missouri Lutheran [a] (112)	Southern Baptist [a] (115)	Sects (263)
Congregationalist	35%	7%	2%	6%	6%	4%	5%	5%	3%	5%
Methodist	19	52	4	7	11	8	6	4	7	6
Episcopalian	13	10	83	7	11	5	7	4	6	4
Disciples of Christ	0	2	*	39	1	0	2	0	3	1
Presbyterian	25	14	7	20	64	8	13	5	11	13
American Lutheran	1	3	2	3	3	70	3	2	3	4
American Baptist	3	3	0	7	3	2	55	2	4	3
Missouri Lutheran	1	1	*	1	*	*	2	75	3	2
Southern Baptist	0	2	0	3	*	0	0	0	53	2
Sects	3	6	2	7	1	3	7	3	7	60
Net percentage gain or loss in membership	+2%	-17%	+40%	-32%	+22%	-5%	-8%	-5%	-34%	-9%

* Less than half of 1%.

[a] Lutheran and Baptist columns have been adjusted to distribute persons who did not indicate whether a previous Lutheran affiliation was with one of the American Lutheran bodies or the Missouri Synod, or who did not indicate whether a previous Baptist affiliation was with American or Southern Baptists. Findings were the same with these persons omitted. They were randomly assigned proportionate to the relative size of the groups in question.

respondent's previous denomination is shown across the top of the table. The denomination to which he presently belongs is shown down the left side. The percentages reflect what has happened to people who at some previous time were members of given denominations. That is, by reading down the Congregationalist column we may see that of those who were formerly Congregationalists, 35 percent still are, while 19 percent are now Methodists, 13 percent have become Episcopalians, and 25 percent changed to Presbyterians. The italicized percentage in each column shows the proportion of a denomination who did not change. Thus the tables show both where people went and where they came from.

It will be seen immediately that stability of membership varies greatly from one denomination to another. The most stable group is the Episcopalians, 83 percent of whom remained Episcopalians. The least stable are the Congregationalists, 65 percent of whom became members of some other denomination. Three other groups differ markedly from the average in their ability to hold their original members. The Disciples of Christ are only slightly better than the Congregationalists in maintaining members, only 39 percent of those who were once Disciples have remained so. On the other hand, the Lutherans, both American and Missouri, are exceeded only by the Episcopalians in retaining members: 70 percent of persons who were once American Lutherans and 75 percent of those who were once Missouri Lutherans, still are. In the rest of the denominations from half to nearly two-thirds of original members have been retained.

But there is a second extremely important question to be asked of these data. The present organizational viability of any denomination is a function not only of holding members, but of *attracting* new ones to make up for losses. We can see in the table that Congregationalists are the weakest in holding their initial members, but *looking across* the Congregationalist row in the table reveals that they are very successful in attracting members from other denominations. Similarly, although the Presbyterians are about average in holding members it can be seen that they are extremely likely to attract new members from other denominations. For example, 25 percent of those who were originally Congregationalists, 20 percent of former Disciples of Christ, and even 13 percent of former sect members are now Presbyterians. On the other hand, the Missouri Lutherans and Southern Baptists seem to hold little attraction for persons from other denominations. These cues revealed by an overall inspection are more readily seen in the row of boldface percentages across the bottom of the table. Here we have compared the present number of members in a denomination with the number originally affiliated with it and computed the net percentage gain or loss. Three denominations have gained at the expense of the others: the Episcopalians have increased their proportion of the Protestant church member population by a startling 40 percent; the Presbyterians have grown by 22 percent; and the Congregationalists have increased by 2 percent. All other denominations have lost ground in the process of member interchange. Hardest hit were the Southern Baptists who declined by 34 percent, the Disciples of Christ lost 32 percent, the Methodists 17 percent, the small sects 9 percent, the American Baptists 8 percent, and the American and Missouri Lutherans have lost 5 percent each. This reveals the importance not only of holding members, but of attracting them. Thus the Congregationalists suffered the most in losing their original membership, but attracted others so successfully that they ended up with a modest overall increase. On the other hand, the Lutheran groups were relatively successful in holding their original members, but were unable to make up their moderate losses from other denominations. The Episcopalians excelled in both ways: they held their original flock better than did the other denominations and they proved a strong attraction to members from other bodies.

It is easy to begin to infer from these data that an important general trend underlies these interdenominational changes: people who change their church tend to move from more conservative bodies to theologically more liberal ones.

In order to demonstrate more fully this trend to liberalism, the data in Table 62 were collapsed into three more general groupings: denominations were classified as liberal, moderate, or conservative. The criterion used to distinguish denominations into these groupings was theology. A restudy of the data shown in Chapters 2 and 3 will reveal that the Congregationalists, Methodists, and Episcopalians form a consistent and distinct *liberal* cluster in terms of the extent of orthodoxy among their members. Similarly, the Disciples of Christ, the Presbyterians, the American Lutherans and the American Baptists form a very similar distinct group which we have called the *moderates*. Finally, it is clear that the Missouri Lutherans, the Southern Baptists, and the

Table 63

DENOMINATIONAL SHIFTS AMONG LIBERAL, MODERATE AND CONSERVATIVE PROTESTANTS *(Church-Member Sample; Protestants only)*

	Respondent's most recent **previous** denomination was:		
	Liberal	Moderate	Conservative
His present denomination is:			
Liberal	75%	23%	14%
Moderate	19	73	19
Conservative	6	4	67
	100%	100%	100%
Number	(883)	(817)	(490)
Net percentage change in membership	**+4%**	**+5%**	**−18%**

various sects constitute a very *conservative* group. Data presented in the next chapter will demonstrate the sharp distinctions among these bodies in all varieties of religious commitment.

Table 63 shows the patterns of denominational turnover within the liberal, moderate, and conservative sectors of American Protestantism. First of all, by comparing the circled percentages along the left to right diagonal of the table it is clear that the liberal and moderate bodies are more successful than the conservatives in holding their original members (75%, 73%, and 67% respectively). But of even greater importance is the fact that

while liberals and moderates exchange members at roughly equivalent rates, they lose very few members to conservative bodies.
Conservatives, on the other hand, lose substantial proportions of
their original members to liberal and moderate bodies. While only
5 percent of the liberals and moderates became conservatives, 33
percent of the conservatives changed to moderate or liberal faiths.
The boldface statistics at the bottom of the table reflect these
changes in terms of the net percentage change in denominational
strength. Here it can be seen that after all the switching has been
accomplished the liberal bodies have 4 percent more members
than they began with, the moderates show a 5 percent gain, but
the *conservatives show an 18 percent loss*. On the basis of these
data it appears that denominational changes among American
Protestants follow a pattern of movement to churches with more
liberal, modernized theologies and away from the churches that
are still foursquare for traditional orthodoxy. This greatly contradicts the prevailing belief that it is the more conservative denominations that are growing fastest these days. Later in this chapter
we shall try to uncover the sources of this myth. But first it seems
useful to gather all of the relevant facts.

Tables 62 and 63 are likely to *underestimate* the extent to
which shifts from conservative to more liberal bodies characterize
denominational changing in our society. As discussed in footnote
4, these data report a person's most recent previous denomination
and not necessarily the denomination in which he was raised. If
the trend is mainly to shift denominations from right to left along
the axis of liberal to conservative theology, then it seems likely
that some persons' most recent former denomination may have
been liberal or moderate although their original denomination was
in the conservative group. A subsequent shift to another liberal or
moderate group is all the data in Tables 62 and 63 will show for
such persons, and the fact that they too moved left from their
original religious heritage would go unnoticed. For this reason
Table 64 reexamines the relationships seen in Table 63. However,
here one's original denomination is based on that of his parents.
Some persons were omitted from the table because their parents

were of mixed Protestant backgrounds,[5] and a number of persons were omitted because they did not provide sufficient information to allow them to be classified.

These data confirm our suspicions. While the data on liberals and moderates are virtually identical with those seen in Table 63, the data on conservatives indicate a considerably greater loss than that shown in Table 63. While 5 percent of those raised as liberals and moderates shifted to conservative bodies, *43 percent* of those raised as conservatives changed to liberal or moderate

Table 64

PARENT'S DENOMINATION AND RESPONDENTS PRESENT DENOMINATION (Church-Member Sample; Protestants only)

	Parents were:		
	Liberals	Moderates	Conservatives
Respondent is:			
Liberal	73%	21%	20%
Moderate	22	74	23
Conservative	5	5	57
Number	(531)	(477)	(328)
Net percentage change from parent's denomination to respondent's present denomination	+3%	+15%	−27%

groups. Thus, while liberals and moderates hold about three-fourths of their original members and exchange the rest while losing only a handful to the conservatives, nearly half of those who began as conservatives defected to the moderates and liberals. The boldface statistics show the net percentage change in denominational membership. The liberals have increased their numbers by 3 percent over what they began with, the moderates are up 15 percent, and the conservatives have shrunk by more

[5] However, relatively few Protestant parents retained different denominations.

than a quarter (27%). If these trends are accurate and continue the conservatives are likely to become an increasingly minor force in American religion.

There is one major impediment to drawing such a conclusion from these data, however. All of these respondents were church members residing in urban, northern California at the time of the study. A great many of the Protestants (and a majority of the conservative Protestants) in the sample had moved to California from small town and rural areas in the midwest and south. There is reason to suppose that leaving one's community ties behind and moving to an urban setting is in itself a break with traditionalism akin to joining a more liberal church. Surely, too, moving to a new area facilitates a change of denomination. Furthermore, the Far West is considered a somewhat less religious area than the rest of the nation (for example, church attendance is considerably lower) and persons may be attracted to it partly for this reason.

Consequently, there are many grounds for questioning the extent to which a portrait of interdenominational change based on Californians accurately reflects trends in the rest of the nation. For these reasons we sought national data.

DENOMINATIONAL MOBILITY NATIONWIDE

Our own national survey did not contain data on the denomination in which persons were raised. Thus, we initiated a search through the hundreds of national surveys that have been conducted for one in which data on original and current denomination had been gathered. For some time the search proved fruitless. Occasionally, such questions were asked, but answers were categorized as Protestant, Catholic, or Jew and thus were unable to shed any light on intra-Protestant changes. Finally, the archives of the National Opinion Research Center yielded a study which provides at least a suggestive basis for inference.[6] As will be pointed out in greater detail below, these data are subject to several important defects and thus all findings must be taken with

[6] We are indebted to Peter H. Rossi, then Director of N.O.R.C., for helping us locate this study and for graciously making it available to us.

considerable caution. Still, even if the findings must necessarily be held quite tentatively, given the complete lack of knowledge on this relatively important matter, some information is better than none.

The N.O.R.C. survey did not ask respondents in what religion they had been raised. However, it did ask the religion of the respondents' fathers. While this introduces some ambiguity, our California findings strongly indicated that no important bias would be introduced by inferring a respondent's religious up-bringing from the religion of his father. For one thing, as reported in footnote 5, mixed denomination couples are relatively uncommon *within* Protestantism. While in marriages which cross Prot-estant-Catholic or Christian-Jewish religious lines many couples tend to retain their original faiths, in marriages of persons from different Protestant denominations both persons tend to end up in the same denomination. The commonness of denominational shifts within Protestantism probably strongly militates against spouses retaining different denominational ties. Furthermore, when Table 64 was reconstructed using only father's denomina-tion to indicate a respondent's original denomination the results were virtually identical with those shown in the table where the faith of both parents was used. Thus father's religion is probably a sufficient basis for inferring the faith in which persons were raised.

A second defect of the data is the relatively small size of the sample (1,469 cases). While it is sufficiently large for many purposes of estimating characteristics of the national population a difficulty arises when it is broken down into many subgroups constituting the various denominations. Thus assertions about the proportions of Presbyterians, for example, who changed to other denominations will be based on a total of sixty-five persons whose fathers were Presbyterian. The question of the extent to which this subgroup of Presbyterians accurately represents all Ameri-can Presbyterians is difficult to answer adequately. However, one important test of the sample's representativeness was possible.

Table 65 compares the proportions of persons in various reli-gious bodies as estimated by both the N.O.R.C. sample and the previously cited survey conducted by the United States Census Bureau. The comparison shows that the N.O.R.C. data very closely approximate the census study. The N.O.R.C. data include a slightly higher proportion of Protestants and a slightly lower proportion of Roman Catholics than does the census study, however the differences are very trivial. At least against this standard the sample seems remarkably representative for its size.

Table 65

A COMPARISON BETWEEN N.O.R.C. SAMPLE AND UNITED STATES CENSUS SAMPLE

	United States Census Bureau Sample Survey * (1957)	N.O.R.C. Sample Survey (SRS-857) (1965)
Protestant	66.2%	68.9%
Baptist	19.7	23.1
Methodist	14.0	13.5
Lutheran	7.1	7.6
Presbyterian	5.6	5.6
Episcopal	⎫	2.9 ⎫
Congregational	⎬ 19.8	1.1 ⎬ 19.1
Other Protestant	⎭	15.1 ⎭
Roman Catholic	25.7	24.5
Jewish	3.2	2.1
Other non-Christian	1.3	1.5
None	2.7	3.0
Not Reported	0.9	0.0
	100.0%	100.0%

* U.S. Bureau of the Census, Current Population Reports, series P-20, no. 79 (Feb. 2, 1958).

An additional difficulty with these data could only be solved in part. Although respondents were not simply identified as "Protestants," the denomination categories into which they were separated were far from adequate. First of all, Baptists constitute a single category and it is not possible to distinguish American from Southern Baptists, let alone separate the various smaller Baptist bodies. Nationally, this may not be as serious as it would be for Californians, however. While in our church-member sample the American Baptists were considerably less likely to be orthodox than were Southern Baptists, in the national data reported in Chapter 2 the differences were somewhat smaller. Still, one would prefer to be able to separate them. Similarly, it is not possible to distinguish among the various Lutheran bodies, and thus the very conservative Missouri Synod Lutherans must be left classified with the more liberal Lutherans of the American Lutheran Church and the Lutheran Church in America. Most serious of all, however, the only Protestant categories are Congregational, Episcopal, Methodist, Presbyterian, Lutheran, and Baptist. *All* remaining Protestant respondents were classified as "other Protestants." Thus, all members of the various smaller conservative and fundamentalist bodies are included in this category, and may even make up the bulk of it, but members of such liberal bodies as the Unitarians, Quakers, Disciples of Christ, and so forth, are also lumped into this residual category. By turning to our own national sample we were able accurately to determine the composition of this "other Protestant" category. We assessed the denominational affiliations of those who did not belong to one of the mainline bodies mentioned above and who would automatically be classed in the "other Protestant" category by N.O.R.C. This analysis revealed virtually an even split between small liberal and moderate bodies, members of which account for 39 percent of the "other" group, and small fundamentalist sects, whose members made up 40 percent of this group. Of the remainder, 7 percent were Latter Day Saints (Mormons), and the other 14 percent were persons who identified themselves as Protestants without a denominational affiliation. Because of this arbitrary mixing of liberals and conservatives, the "other Protestant" category is unintelligible in terms of left or right, and the extreme liberal and conservative ends of the American Protestant spectrum are lost to our analysis. This category is included in Table 66, but had to be dropped from subsequent tables. Finally, for lack of cases it was necessary to exclude non-whites from the data.

Having warned of the various defects in these data, we may now see what can be inferred from them about denominational changing among contemporary Americans. It is immediately evident in Table 66 that changing denomination is not peculiar to

Table 66

DENOMINATIONAL CHANGE (Nationwide, whites only)

		Father's religion was:										
	Catholic	Jewish	Other Non-Christian	None	Unknown	Congre-gational	Episco-palian	Metho-dist	Presby-terian	Lutheran	Baptist	Other Protestant
Number:	(311)	(28)	(29)	(52)	(117)	(15)	(31)	(167)	(65)	(123)	(193)	(152)
Respondent's religion is:												
Catholic	86%	0%	7%	8%	31%	13%	3%	7%	5%	7%	2%	4%
Jewish	0	89	0	0	3	0	7	0	0	0	0	0
Other Non-Christian	*	4	28	4	*	0	3	1	0	0	0	3
None	1	7	10	18	4	0	7	2	5	1	2	4
Congregationalist	1	0	3	0	2	54	0	2	3	0	0	0
Episcopalian	1	0	0	2	4	0	55	2	9	2	1	2
Methodist	2	0	7	16	10	7	6	57	6	9	7	7
Presbyterian	3	0	0	4	7	13	3	5	51	3	4	7
Lutheran	1	0	0	4	3	0	10	4	3	65	2	6
Baptist	2	0	7	13	16	0	3	7	9	1	72	16
Other Protestant	3	0	38	31	20	13	3	11	9	12	10	53
Net percentage gain or loss in membership	−*	−4%	−34%	−31%	x	+8%	+29%	−7%	+15%	−12%	+3%	+18%

* Less than half of 1%.

x Since the religious affiliation of all respondents was known there was no such thing as an unknown category, for present religion. In computing net losses and gains for other bodies persons who did not know their father's religion were not counted.

California Protestants, more than 40 percent of American Protestants are not in the same denomination as were their fathers. By contrast, shifts across Protestant-Catholic or Christian-Jewish lines are much less common. Eighty-six percent of the Catholics and 89 percent of the Jews have remained in their respective faiths. Similarly, only small proportions of Protestants have crossed into Catholicism and only a handful have become Jews.

The least stable religious conditions among Americans are to be born into a non-Christian faith other than Judaism, only 28 percent of such persons have retained their original faith, or to be born into no faith at all, only 18 percent of whom have stayed outside some religious affiliation.

Among Protestants, the Baptists and the Lutherans have retained the largest proportion of their original members (72% and 65% respectively), while there are no important differences among the other Protestant bodies all of whom have retained from 51 percent to 57 percent of their born members. There is a suggestion in the data that persons from non-Christian (other than Jewish) backgrounds or from no religious background are strongly recruited into fundamentalist Protestant bodies: 38 percent of the former and 31 percent of the latter are now classified in the "other Protestant" category. This category is very ambiguous, of course, and perhaps these people are being recruited into very liberal bodies such as the Unitarians. However, some speculations later in this chapter will heighten the likelihood that it is the fundamentalists who account for these particular "other Protestant" figures. On the other hand, the movement of 13 percent of the Congregationalists and 11 percent of the Methodists into this "other" category might well reflect recruitment into the very liberal Protestant bodies. Oddly enough Episcopalians are less likely than all other Protestants except Baptists to become Roman Catholics. The liturgical similarity between Roman and Anglican faiths has long led to the belief that member exchange was relatively high between the two. However, the table also shows that Catholics are less likely to become Episcopalians than they are to become Methodists, Presbyterians, or Baptists. This suggests that perhaps the notion of an Episcopalian-Catholic affinity is false. Indeed, in these data Episcopalians are more likely to turn Jewish than Catholic.

We have seen earlier in the church-member sample that ability to hold original members is only one part of the process, churches must also show an ability to attract members from other bodies. Thus, the boldface percentages across the bottom of the table must be examined in order to judge the net effects of denomination-switching. These figures show that Roman Catholicism seems in a state of virtual equilibrium, when their losses and gains are compared the Catholic church shows a trivial loss of less than .5 of 1 percent. Jews also are close to a balance: showing a net loss of 4 percent. Non-Christian bodies, and the unchurched categories suffer the greatest losses: the former have lost 34 percent and the latter 31 percent of their original affiliates. Within Protestantism the trends are strikingly similar to those found among California church members. In California, three Protestant bodies showed increases: the Episcopalians, Presbyterians, and Congregationalists, in that order. In the national data these same bodies also show an increase in their net membership and the rank order is the same as in California. Episcopalians have grown by 29 percent nationwide, Presbyterians by 15 percent, and the Congregationalists by 8 percent. The only difference between California and the nation as a whole is in the growth of the Baptists. In the California sample all Baptist groups showed losses in total membership, while nationwide they exhibit a 3 percent increase. As we shall discuss shortly this may stem from having originally unchurched persons in the data (16% of whom became Baptists), and because of recruitment from the small sects included in the "other Protestant" category. This last group, a confusing mixture of fundamentalist and ultra-liberal bodies, has also shown growth: 18 percent. We shall later suggest that some of this growth is concentrated among the liberal bodies included in this category.

Overall, however, these data closely approximate our earlier California findings, and thus suggest that California is not really so different after all. Still, it is very difficult to determine trends in denominational changing among Protestants in this table. For one thing the ambiguity of the "other Protestant" category clouds the issue, and besides the table is really too complex. In Table 67, however, "other Protestants" have been excluded, and denominations have been grouped into liberal, moderate, and conservative clusters. The liberals include the Congregationalists, the Episcopalians, and the Methodists. The moderates comprise the Presbyterians and Lutherans, while the Baptists make up the conservative group. As we have seen, a denomination's present

Table 67

TRENDS IN PROTESTANT DENOMINATIONAL SHIFTS
(National N.O.R.C. Sample; whites only)

	Respondent's father was:		
	A liberal Protestant	A moderate Protestant	A conserva- tive Protestant
Respondent is:			
A liberal Protestant	80%	17%	10%
A moderate Protestant	12	79	7
A conservative Protestant	8	4	83
Number	(169)	(151)	(168)
Net percentage change in membership	+4%	+1%	−5%

membership is a function both of maintaining original members and of recruiting from other denominations. The table shows that while conservatives do slightly better in holding their original membership, they do a bit less well than do liberals and moderates at attracting new members. Thus, as shown in the boldface figures at the bottom of the table, while the liberals accomplished a net percentage increase of 4 percent, and the moderates gained by 1 percent, the conservatives lost 5 percent from the total with which they began. Thus these national data provide a cautious confirmation of the trends revealed in the California data: in the process of Protestant church-switching liberal and moderate bodies are gaining membership at the expense of the conservatives. However, the extent of gains and losses produced by this trend of changing from conservative to more moderate denominations is considerably smaller over the nation as a whole. This suggests that there is indeed something about moving to California that adds impetus to such change. Upon reflection it seems likely that this right-to-left swing in American denominational affiliation might be associated with urbanization, particularly outside the South, long noted as a conservative Protestant bastion.

Table 68 allows this conjecture to be examined. Respondents have been separated according to whether they reside in urban areas or small town and rural areas. In addition Southerners have been separated from Northerners. The boldface percentages across the bottom of the table tell a revealing story: the shift from more to less conservative bodies is greatest among persons who live in northern, urban areas. However, even in southern urban areas conservatives are losing members (although here liberals are losing too and only the moderate bodies show gains). Furthermore, liberal bodies would appear to be growing in both northern and southern small towns and rural areas as well, while conservatives appear to be increasing *only* in northern small town and rural areas.

It must be recognized that these data are based upon relatively few cases and thus must be treated with extreme caution. However, the consistent pattern revealed and the fact that it is congruent with what much more solid evidence showed for California, lends the findings at least a certain plausibility.

If we accept the trends shown in both the national and the California data, several questions automatically arise. First of all, membership figures reported annually to the National Council of Churches have long shown that the conservative churches are growing faster than the moderate and liberal bodies. But our data suggest that the conservative bodies ought to account for a smaller proportion of church members each year. There seem several possible explanations for this contradiction. For one thing, it has recently become apparent that church membership statistics are extremely unreliable.[7] It may be that the figures showing a faster rate of growth by conservative bodies are simply

[7] For a summary of critiques of church statistics see: Charles Y. Glock and Rodney Stark, *Religion and Society in Tension* (Chicago: Rand McNally, 1965), ch. 4.

Table 68
DENOMINATIONAL CHANGE BY REGION AND BY RURAL/URBAN (National Sample; whites only)

| | Urban areas | | | | | | Small town and rural areas | | | | | |
| | Northern | | | Southern | | | Northern | | | Southern | | |
	Liberal	Mod-erate	Conser-vative	Liberal	Mod-erate	Conser-vative	Liberal	Mod-erate	Conser-vative	Liberal	Mod-erate	Conser-vative
Liberal	80	15%	11%	69%	25%	6%	87%	14%	6%	80%	*	12%
Moderate	18	84	11	12	60	12	9	84	6	4	*	0
Conservative	2	1	78	19	15	82	4	2	88	16	*	88
Number	(66)	(74)	(36)	(32)	(20)	(59)	(46)	(48)	(15)	(25)	(9 *)	(58)
Net percentage change in mem-bership	+3%	+5%	-17%	-3%	+15%	-3%	+4%	-6%	+7%	+16%		-2%

* Too few cases for stable percentage.

in error. Indeed, the Southern Baptists admitted that a campaign a few years ago to locate inactive members showed that at least one-fourth of those persons carried on their membership rolls, and reported in their statistics, no longer belong to a Baptist church in the community where they live.[8] In collecting the data on church members for the present study we also found considerable deadwood on church rolls.[9] We concluded that churches are typically very prompt in adding new names to their rolls but are very lax about removing persons who have died, moved away, or quit the church. Thus all church statistics are considerably inflated. However, through this process churches that lose a larger proportion of their initial membership ought to accrue the larger proportion of deadwood on their current membership rolls. The statistics of the conservative churches ought to be more erroneous than those of the liberal and moderate bodies. Thus the conservative churches may have been celebrating a paper empire, and while they thought they were doing better than other denominations they may actually have been doing worse.

But there is a second possible process that may also be at work. Although virtually all Americans claim a denominational affiliation, only somewhat over half claim to belong to a specific congregation or parish of this denomination. Thus a great many Americans are in this sense unchurched. It is also the case that actual membership in a congregation is highly related to social class, church membership is predominately a middle and upper class affair.[10] Given the rising affluence of postwar America with the increasing size of the middle class it is probably the case that many new people moving into the middle classes are taking up church membership (as opposed to merely claiming a denomination). It is also true that persons moving into the middle classes tend to have a prior denominational affiliation with the more conservative churches. Consequently, when they take up congre-

---

[8] *Christian Century*, LXIX (October 8, 1952), pp. 1148–1149.

[9] See the Methodological Appendix in Charles Y. Glock and Rodney Stark, *Christian Beliefs and Anti-Semitism* (New York: Harper and Row, 1966).

[10] This was touched upon in Chapter 4, and will be considered in some detail in the second volume in this study.

gational membership it is likely to be in a conservative body. Thus, in terms of members of actual congregations, rather than mere denominational acknowledgement, the conservative ranks may be filling from newly affluent lower class persons, while the established middle classes are moving out. It will be recalled that in Table 66 the Baptists showed an overall 3 percent increase in total membership. Subsequently, in Tables 67 and 68, where the "other Protestant" category was omitted they consistently showed a net loss. Since the smaller fundamentalist Protestant sects are included in this category it suggests that a prime source of Baptist recruitment is from such bodies, which is consistent with the hypothesis of an influx from the unchurched upwardly mobile lower classes, many of whom would previously have had a fundamentalist affiliation. It is also consistent with our overall picture of a conservative to liberal trend in church switching. The conservative category in our data, which is made up of a composite of Baptist bodies, is less conservative than are these small fundamentalist groups. Such a movement from the sects to the Baptists is a move in a liberal direction.

Furthermore, the Baptists show considerable power in attracting members from those without an original denomination ("none") and from among those who did not know what religion their father was. Such a pattern is also consistent with our hypothesis that the Baptists are activating unchurched persons. But there are two basic types of people who are unchurched. One type is basically a phenomenon of low social class—people who are simply outside most of society's institutions, the isolated, often itinerant, extremely impoverished underdogs. Such persons typically have a basic belief in religion. The other type is outside the church through conscious choice, they have rejected the basic tenets of religion. It is the underdog type that ought to be most readily recruitable by conservative churches. This is reflected in the ability of the Baptists to recruit persons from the "none" and "unknown" categories. Similarly such persons ought to be quite recruitable by the small sects. Table 66 shows that 31 percent of the "nones" and 20 percent of the "unknowns" have joined groups in the "other Protestant" class. But it seems also plausible that many persons raised by parents who have rejected formal church affiliation out of theological conviction might join very liberal bodies. The fact that persons from the "none" category are about two and one-half times more likely to become "other Protestants" than to become Baptists suggests that this is the case. Some of these people are joining the Unitarians, Quakers, and similar liberal bodies.

But there is another apparent puzzle revealed by our findings. The trend to liberalism ought to be causing a considerable expansion in the size of the liberal and moderate denomination in terms of enrolled members at the congregation level. But this seems not to be happening. These bodies have not reported substantial increases in membership. This seeming contradiction suggests the following cycle is operating in American church affiliation. Persons moving into the middle classes are activated by conservative congregations. However, the more established middle and upper classes are moving into moderate and liberal denominations—the newly-churched conservatives would be expected to follow them as their middle class status has crystalized. But in addition, a good many people who begin life as liberals must be dropping their congregational affiliation for a secular life, although so far they probably mainly claim a liberal denominational affiliation when asked. Thus the leftward trend in denominational switching may not stop once people reach the most liberal denominations, but may carry many on out of the churches altogether. This hypothesized exodus is lent plausibility by findings in previous chapters that the liberal denominations fare badly in generating member commitment even among those who are presently upon their congregational rolls.

Of course such a process cannot continue indefinitely. Eventually nearly everyone would have flowed through the denominations and on out of the churches. In the next chapter we shall assess this as a long-run possibility. But in the shorter run, these trends prevent a fairly immediate threat to the conservative bodies. If our data are reliable, it would appear that members of the conservative bodies are slowly draining away.

Chapter 11

ARE WE ENTERING A POST-CHRISTIAN ERA?*

Write the things which thou hast seen, and the things which are, and the things which shall be hereafter.
Revelation 1:19 (A.V.)

Perhaps at no prior time since the conversion of Paul has the future of Christianity seemed so uncertain. Clearly, a profound revolution in religious thought is sweeping through the churches. But where will it lead: is this a moment of great promise or peril for the future of Christianity?

Some observers believe we have already entered a post-Christian era and that the current upheavals are the death throes of a doomed religion. Yet many theologians interpret these same signs as the promise of an era of renewed religious vigor. They foresee the possibility of a reconstructed and unified church which will recapture its relevance to contemporary life. A great many others, both clerical and lay, are simply mystified. In the face of rapid changes and conflicting claims for the future they hardly know whether to prepare for the church to rise triumphant or to administer the last rites to the faith. Probably the majority of Christians think the whole matter has been greatly exaggerated; that the present excitement too shall pass away and the churches will continue pretty much as before.

The most singular feature of the current debate about the future of Christianity has been the almost total lack of evidence. The arguments have been based on speculation, hope, and even

* A number of our colleagues made careful and extensive criticisms of the initial draft of this chapter. We are indebted to Jay Demerath, Langdon Gilkey, Andrew J. Greeley, Phillip E. Hammond, Benton Johnson, Gerhard Lenski, Martin E. Marty, James A. Pike, David Riesman, Guy E. Swanson, and Milton Yinger. They deserve credit for many improvements and for saving us from several important errors. We alone are responsible for all errors of judgment and interpretation which remain.

temperament, but rarely on fact. Mainly this has been because so few hard facts about contemporary religion have been available. Our own data do not entirely fill this vacuum. Still, what we have learned in the preceding chapters provides a number of clues about the trends in religious commitment and permits a cautious assessment of the present controversy. In this concluding chapter we shall try to interpret these trends.

Any attempt to characterize the shifting patterns of American religion is extremely difficult. Partly this is because the situation is in such a state of flux that what seems certain today may be false tomorrow. But it is also because it is difficult, if not impossible, to be dispassionate about anything concerning religion. Inevitably, personal feelings intrude and influence judgments about what is happening. Our conclusions will probably be partly governed by our particular viewpoint. But the only alternative to risking a distorted judgment is to say nothing at all.

What then are the main features of the changing character of American Christianity? The evidence leads us to two conclusions: the religious beliefs which have been the bedrocks of Christian faith for nearly two millennia are on their way out; this may very well be the dawn of a post-Christian era.

While many Americans are still firmly committed to the traditional supernatural conceptions of a personal God, a Divine Saviour, and the promise of eternal life, the trend is away from these convictions. Although we must anticipate an extended period of doubt, the new reformation in religious thought reflects the fact that a demythologized modernism is overwhelming the traditional, Christ-centered, mystical faith.

Of course rejection of the supernatural tenets of Christianity is not a modern phenomenon. Through the ages men have challenged these beliefs. But they have never found appreciable popular support. Until now the vast majority of people have remained unshaken in their faith in the otherworldly premises of Christianity.

But the modern skeptics are not going unnoticed, nor are their criticisms being rejected out of hand. For the modern skeptics are not the apostates, village atheists, or political revolutionaries of old. The leaders of today's challenge to traditional beliefs are principally theologians, those in whose care the church entrusts its sacred teachings. It is not philosophers or scientists, but the greatest theologians of our time who are saying "God is dead," or that notions of a "God out there" are antiquated. And their views are becoming increasingly popular.

Although only a minority of church members so far reject or doubt the existence of some kind of personal God or the divinity of Jesus, a near majority reject such traditional articles of faith as Christ's miracles, life beyond death, the promise of the second coming, the virgin birth, and an overwhelming majority reject the existence of the Devil. This overall picture is subject to considerable variation among the denominations. Old-time Christianity remains predominant in some Protestant bodies such as the Southern Baptists and the various small sects. But in most of the mainline Protestant denominations, and to a considerable extent among Roman Catholics, doubt and disbelief in historic Christian theology abound. In some denominations the doubters far outnumber the firm believers.

The signs of this revolution in religious thought are compelling. Still, we have no certain evidence that fewer theologians a generation ago doubted traditional Christian doctrines. Nor can we prove that the forebears of today's Christians were less inclined to doubt these doctrines. There simply is no reliable evidence on the state of faith in past times. Nevertheless, we are convinced that the widespread doubt of traditional Christian tenets is a recent development, that previous generations have been more prone to traditional convictions.

What evidence there is supports this assumption. The data on denominational switching presented in Chapter 10 do not bear directly on inter-generational changes in religious belief. Yet, if there has been an erosion of traditional faith we would expect people to be shifting from denominations which have retained unswerving commitment to that faith into denominations with more demythologized positions. This is exactly what we did find. Because these trends do not directly indicate changes in religious outlooks, they do not prove the case. But they are very consistent with it.

More direct evidence of an erosion in orthodox belief is provided by contrasts in the proportions of orthodox believers in different age groups. In an analysis reported elsewhere, based on our church-member sample, it was found that age made very little difference in the proportion subscribing to traditional beliefs among respondents fifty years of age or older.[1] Similarly, among those *under* fifty, orthodoxy differed little by age. But Christians over fifty are considerably more likely than younger persons to hold orthodox views. The difference occurs in every denomination and is quite substantial. These findings suggest an important generational break with traditional religion and that it occurred rather recently.[2]

The existence of a growing erosion in religious commitment is further corroborated by a Gallup Poll report issued just as this book was going to press.[3] The most recent Gallup findings indicated a continuation of the downward trend in American church attendance which began in the late 1950's. This decline has been particularly sharp among young adults; the proportion of them who attend weekly dropped 11 percentage points between 1958 and 1966. Furthermore, the Gallup interviewers found that Americans overwhelmingly *believe* that religion is losing its influence in contemporary life. While in 1957 only 14 percent of the nation's Christians thought religion was losing its influence and 69 percent thought it was increasing, ten years later 57 percent thought religion was losing and only 23 percent perceived faith to be

[1] Rodney Stark, "Age and Faith," *Sociological Analysis,* in press.

[2] The inter-generational break consistently occurs between those who grew up since the beginning of World War II, those who were 25 or less in 1940, and those who were raised in a pre-war America. In this and in many other ways World War II seems to mark a watershed between the older America of small town and rural living (or stable urban neighborhood), and the contemporary America of highly mobile, urban life and the development of a mass culture.

[3] American Institute of Public Opinion, press release of April 11, 1967.

gaining. Obviously, these appraisals could be inaccurate, for the respondents were being asked to make an expert judgment. Still, taken as a reflection of their own personal attitudes towards religion, this would seem to mark an enormous loss of confidence in religious institutions during the past decade.

Aside from this statistical evidence, there are numerous more easily observable signs that a religious revolution is taking place. The radical changes in the Roman Catholic Church flowing from the reforms of Pope John XXIII and Vatican II are perhaps the most obvious indications. But of equal significance is the ecumenical movement. As we have suggested earlier, the prevailing differences in doctrinal outlook presently offer insurmountable obstacles to the unification of every Christian denomination. But while such differences probably precluded all prospects of unification several generations ago, today doctrinal barriers have broken down sufficiently between some groups so that mergers have already taken place and more are obviously in the offing. The mergers are taking place among denominations with the least residual commitment to traditional faith. More traditional denominations remain resistant to the prospects of ecumenism. Thus it seems clear that a loss of concern for traditional doctrine is a precondition for ecumenism, and thus that the success of ecumenism today is a sign of the trend away from historic creeds.

These major signs of the depth and scope of religious change are accompanied by a spate of minor clues: the popularity of Bishop Robinson's *Honest to God*, and Harvey Cox's *The Secular City;* the widespread discussion of "death of God" theology in the mass media; the profound changes in the Westminster Confession recently adopted by the Presbyterian Church. All of these are compelling evidence of ferment. Nor is this primarily a Protestant phenomenon. Almost daily the press reports nuns leaving their orders because they believe they can more effectively pursue their missions from a secular circumstance. Priests advocate "the pill." The number of persons taking up religious vocations has been dropping sharply. Laymen ponder Tielhard de Chardin as seriously as Protestants reflect on Bonhoeffer. A leading Jesuit theologian is quoted in *Newsweek* as admitting "It is difficult to say in our age what the divinity of Christ can mean."

The seeds of this revolution were planted a long time ago. Since Kierkegaard, the "death of God" has been proclaimed, albeit subtly and not in such precise language, by the theologians who have counted most. It is only because what has been said privately for years within formal theology is now being popularized that the religious revolution seems such a recent phenomenon.[4] Perhaps this is the pattern of all revolutions, they only become apparent when elite opinion achieves mass appeal.

The heart of this revolution is the demise of what for nearly 2,000 years has been proclaimed as the core of Christian faith: a literal interpretation of the phrase "Christ crucified, risen, coming again." A great many conservative Christians, of course, not only reject the possibility of a Christian faith not predicated on the literal truth of traditional tenets, but deny that any such changes are making substantial headway. However, a large number of churchmen, and certainly many others outside the church, will consider what we have said so far as "old hat." Both the fact of the current revolution and its demythologizing character are taken for granted in many theological circles. But for all that we believe that the obvious, in this instance, is terribly important—perhaps vastly more important than contemporary churchmen recognize.

---

[4] During recent attempts to try him for heresy, Episcopalian Bishop James A. Pike defended himself as having merely told the laity what the clergy have taken for granted for years. Bishop Pike charged that modernized interpretations of doctrine which are commonplace in theological journals have been kept secret from ordinary church members in the interests of harmony. While it seems quite true that the new theology has rarely been preached from the pulpit in Episcopalian churches, which supports Bishop Pike's contentions, nevertheless the average Episcopalian has adopted these modernized views. Indeed, the majority of Episcopalian church members in our sample hold theological views quite similar to Bishop Pike's. This presents the ironic picture of Sunday services where both pastor and laymen reject or at least doubt the theological assumptions of the creeds they recite and the rituals in which they participate, but never acknowledge this fact.

In most of the commentary on the major transformations of our religious institutions the key terms are change, renewal, and improvement. The fact that a massive change in belief is taking place is not characterized as a transition from belief to unbelief, but as a shift from one form of belief to another. The theologians who are leading this process do not regard themselves as pallbearers at the funeral of God. It is not the end of the Christian era, but the dawn of a new and more profound Christian period that they anticipate.

But the subtleties of what is being proposed in place of the old beliefs seem elusive. As sociologists, we find it difficult to imagine a Christian church without Jesus Christ as Divine Saviour, without a God conceived of in personal terms, without the promise of eternal life. The "New Breed" of theologians, as we understand them, are telling us we are wrong; that we rigidly identify Christianity with an old-fashioned fundamentalism which modern Christian thought has long discarded. While we would admit that the religious beliefs that are declining in their importance are traditional ones, we find it difficult to grasp the substance of the alternatives. Conceptions of God as ultimate concern, as love, as poetry, as the divine essence in all of us—the ground of our being—have powerful aesthetic, and rhetorical appeal. But how do they differ from humanism? More important, can such conceptions induce the kind of commitment necessary to keep the church, as an organization, alive?

For some contemporary churchmen the new theology does in fact mean the eventual abandonment of today's church and its replacement by a still vaguely defined spiritual community. But the vast majority anticipate no such thing. They expect the new theology to be effectively accommodated in the present institutional church, although they recognize that this will require some alterations in its present organization and modes of operation.

But so far the new theology has not basically altered the structure, form, or functioning of the institutional church. The churches continue to predicate their structure and activities upon a conception of a judging, personal, active God, *whether or not* the theological views predominate among clergy and laity still conceive of God in these terms. Historically, the central concern of the churches has been the relationship between man and God. Part of their efforts have been directed to propitiating this active God, to teach what must be done to escape his wrath and secure his blessings. Such common religious terms and phrases as praise, worship, seeking comfort and guidance, bringing the unconverted to faith, seeking forgiveness for sins, all presuppose the existence of a conscious, revealing, judging God who intervenes in human affairs. An elaborate conception of God and his commandments is the raison d'être for church worship services, mission societies, adult Bible classes, baptism, communion, and for all the other primary functions and forms as they are presently conducted by the churches.

Admittedly, there have been some superficial alterations. There have been various liturgical experiments. The Mass is sometimes now recited in English rather than Latin. Pastors have undoubtedly made some changes in the content of their sermons. But, by and large, the churches are still organized and conducted as they have been in the past, on the assumptions of an orthodox theology despite the fact that these assumptions are widely doubted. The traditional creeds are still recited—"I believe in God the Father almighty, maker of heaven and earth . . ."—and the old hymns regularly sung—"I know that my Redeemer liveth." There has been no substantial change in the offering of the sacraments, or of the character of the activities conducted at the congregational level. And, with possibly some rare exceptions, there are no loud, nor even soft, cries from the pulpit that Christ did not walk on water or that God does not see and hear all.

The general absence of institutional change does not reflect a clergy that is more committed than the laity to traditional tenets. On the contrary rejection of traditional Christian supernaturalism is perhaps even more widespread among the clergy than among the laity and follows essentially the same pattern of variation by denomination.[5] However, even if they would like to alter

[5] A recent study comparing our findings on church members with national samples of clergy showed that laymen and clergymen in a given denomination are nearly identically distributed on questions of belief. For example,

the forms of the church on the basis of their new theology, liberal ministers are not likely to find their congregations ready to permit it. This is because supporters of the old theology still persist in all denominations, and as we shall consider shortly, persist most commonly among the most active laymen. Thus the liberal pastor faces formidable restraints. His religious convictions might dispose him to reforms, to delete, for example, references to traditional supernaturalism in the worship service, or to preach the new theology from the pulpit and teach it in Sunday school. However, he is unlikely to have a congregation that would tolerate such changes. Indeed, even in congregations where orthodox members are in the minority, such changes are unlikely because the minority will oppose them vigorously, while the plain fact, as we shall see, is that the more liberal members are not likely to care much one way or the other.

It is the discrepancy between institutional inertia and theological revolution which we suspect presents the churches with growing peril. Can the old institutional forms of the church continue to elicit commitment and support from persons whose theological outlook is no longer represented in these forms—or at least maintain sufficient support until such time as the theological revolution is so widespread that it is possible to make institutional changes? But perhaps an even more serious question is whether a Christianity without Christ as a literal Saviour can survive in *any* institutional form.

Our data provide no final answer to these questions. They do,

---

while 34 percent of Methodist laymen and 92 percent of Missouri Synod Lutheran laymen accept the virgin birth, 28 percent of Methodist clergy and 90 percent of Missouri Lutheran clergy accept this article of faith. See: Jeffrey K. Hadden, "A Protestant Paradox—Divided They Merge," *Trans-Action* (July/August, 1967), pp. 63–69. Similar results were recently reported when items on belief taken from our questionnaire were used in a study of clergymen participating in a national meeting of the National Council of Churches of Christ. The study, conducted by Glen W. Trimble (reported in *Information Service*, May, 1967) showed that clergymen at this gathering were somewhat less likely to hold traditional views than were members of their various denominations. However, the differences among denominations were very similar to those found in our study.

however, provide some important clues as to what will happen should future developments follow the present course. As they are now constituted, it is evident that belief in traditional Christian doctrines is vital to other kinds of religious commitment. While the churches continue to be organized on the basis of traditional orthodoxy, persons who lack the beliefs which are needed to make such organization meaningful are falling away from religious institutions: *a general corrosion of commitment presently accompanies the acceptance of a modernized, liberal theology.*

Table 69 shows that among both Protestants (in every instance but one) and Roman Catholics, other aspects of religious commitment are very strongly related to orthodoxy. The highly orthodox are also much more likely to be ritually involved in the church, and far surpass the less orthodox on devotionalism, religious experience, knowledge, and particularism. Only on ethicalism among Protestants is the pattern reversed. By a slight margin it is the least orthodox who are more likely to hold the ideals of Christian ethics. Clearly, a loss of orthodoxy is very powerfully related to a loss of religiousness on these other aspects of piety as well.

Nevertheless, we recognize the fact that it could be convincingly argued that devotionalism, religious experience, knowledge, particularism, and perhaps even ritual involvement are not intrinsically necessary to the existence of Christian institutions. The fact that these forms of commitment decline as traditional belief is eroded could be interpreted as reflecting changes in modes of religious expression rather than a decline in commitment to religious institutions. After all, the new theology implies not only a departure from old time supernaturalism, but from other forms of commitment which are undergirded by supernaturalism. The clergy of the new reformation hardly expect to produce an outbreak of speaking in unknown tongues among their adherents.

However, it is quite implausible to speak simply of change rather than of decline unless religious institutions retain a laity committed in *some* fashion. On purely practical grounds, the churches cannot survive as formal organizations unless a sufficient proportion of persons participate in the life of the church

Table 69

THE IMPACT OF ORTHODOX BELIEF ON OTHER ASPECTS OF COMMITMENT (Church-Member Sample)

	Orthodoxy Index		
	Low	Medium	High
Percentage high on Ritual Involvement			
Protestants	19	39	71
Catholics	19	36	55
Percentage high on Devotionalism			
Protestants	20	49	79
Catholics	18	58	80
Percentage high on Religious Experience			
Protestants	25	57	86
Catholics	29	49	70
Percentage high on Religious Knowledge			
Protestants	15	19	46
Catholics	0	5	7
Percentage high on Particularism			
Protestants	9	25	60
Catholics	15	28	40
Percentage high on Ethicalism			
Protestants **	47	46	42
Catholics	48	48	56
Number of cases on which percentages are based.*			
Protestants	595	729	705
Catholics	64	115	304

* With trivial variations all computations in these tables are based on this same number of cases.

** Members of Protestant sects are excluded from these computations as explained in Chapter 3.

and provide it with financial support. Without funds or members surely the churches would be empty shells awaiting demolition.

The data in Table 70 suggest that this is at least a plausible version of the future. Among both Protestants and Catholics, church attendance is very powerfully related to orthodoxy. Only 15 percent of those Protestants with the most fully modernized religious beliefs attend church every week, while 59 percent of those who have retained traditional orthodox views do so. Among

Table 70

THE IMPACT OF ORTHODOX BELIEF ON ORGANIZATIONAL SUPPORT FOR THE CHURCH *
(Church-Member Sample)

| | Orthodoxy Index | | |
	Low	Medium	High
Percentage who attend church every week			
Protestants	15	31	59
Catholics	27	60	82
Percentage who belong to one or more church organizations			
Protestants	46	61	72
Catholics	14	24	46
Percentage who contribute $7.50 or more per week to their church			
Protestants	17	23	44
Catholics	2	4	8
Percentage of Catholics who contribute $4 or more per week to their church	13	19	26

* With trivial variations all computations are based on the number of cases shown in Table 69.

Catholics the contrast is 27 percent versus 82 percent. Similarly, the table shows that membership in one or more church organizations is strongly related to orthodoxy. Finally, financial support for the churches is mainly provided by those with orthodox views. These findings are powerful within all Protestant denominations as well, and when the social class of church members was taken into account the relationships between orthodoxy and institutional support for the churches were even stronger.

These data strongly testify that the institutional church, predicated as it is on traditional theological concepts, tends to lose its meaning and its ability to move men as these concepts become outmoded. Consequently, if the erosion of traditional beliefs continues, as presumably it will, so long as the church remains locked in its present institutional forms it stands in ever-increasing danger of both moral and literal bankruptcy. At the moment, the liberal denominations are particularly vulnerable because the demise of traditional theology and a concomitant drop in other aspects of commitment is already considerably widespread in these bodies.

However, it seems clear that the solution is not a return to orthodoxy. In coming days many conservative Christians will undoubtedly argue and work for such an about-face. We judge their prospects for success as minuscule. The current reformation in religious thought appears irrevocable, and it seems as likely that we can recover our innocence in these matters as that we can again believe the world flat or that lightning is a palpable manifestation of God's wrath.

Is there any way the likely impending triumph of liberal theology can be translated into the regeneration of religious institutions, anticipated by the liberal clergy? Or must it inevitably lead to the demise of organized faith? It is here the future is most murky. The alternatives to orthodoxy being advocated by the new theologians and their supporters are still relatively formless and inchoate. It is too soon to know just how they will evolve. However, their central thrust seems to be towards the ethical rather than the mystical.

But this is more than a change in emphasis. The ethics of the new theologies differ sharply from the old. No longer are Christian ethics defined as matters of personal holiness or the rejection of private vices, but they are directed towards social justice, with the creation of a humane society. As Langdon Gilkey put it recently, there has been a "shift in Christian ethical concern from personal holiness to love of neighbor as the central obligation, if not the essence, of Christianity . . . [a concern] with a man's attitudes and behavior in relation to his neighbor in the social community."[6] In the new ethical perspective the individual is not neglected for the sake of the group, but the whole question of what is ethical is freed from the confines of the individual and seen as integral to the social situation in which persons are embedded. The long Christian quest to save the world through

[6] Langdon Gilkey, "Social and Intellectual Sources of Contemporary Protestant Theology in America," *Daedalus* (Winter, 1967), p. 73.

individual salvation has shifted to questions of how to reform society directly.

Consequently, the new theology is manifested less in what one believes about God than in what one believes about goodness, justice, and compassion. A depersonalized and perhaps intuitively understood God may be invoked by these theologies, but what seems to count most is not how one prepares for the next life—the reality of which the new theology seems to deny—but what one does to realize the kingdom of God on earth.

As we have seen earlier, ethicalism may provide a substitute for orthodoxy among some modern Christians. Ethicalism—the importance placed on "Loving thy neighbor" and "Doing good for others"—is more prevalent in denominations where orthodoxy is least common (recall Chapter 3). Furthermore, individual Christian church members whose religious beliefs are the least orthodox are slightly more inclined to score high on ethicalism than are the most orthodox (Table 69).

But from an institutional point of view, is ethicalism a satisfactory substitute for orthodoxy? Can ethical concern generate and sustain the kinds of practical commitment—financial support and personal participation—which the churches need to survive?

If the churches continue their present policy of business as usual, the answer is probably no. The ethically oriented Christian seems to be deterred rather than challenged by what he finds in church. The more a man is committed to ethicalism the less likely he is to contribute funds or participate in the life of the church. We suspect he is also less likely, in the long run, to remain a member.

As we interpret our data, a decline in church support and participation is a function both of a decline in orthodoxy and a reaction against the present nature of the churches by those who have taken up an ethical conception of Christianity. Tables 71 and 72 show the joint effects of orthodoxy and ethicalism on financial contributions and church attendance. Table 71 shows that among Protestants the more a church member is committed to ethics the less likely he is to contribute money to his church,

Table 71

ORTHODOXY, ETHICALISM, AND CONTRIBUTIONS TO THE CHURCH (Church-Member Sample)

	Ethicalism Index		
	High	Medium	Low
	Percentage who contribute $7.50 or more per week to their church		
Protestants			
Orthodoxy Index			
High	38	43	58
	(304)	(240)	(111)
Medium	18	25	43
	(333)	(321)	(44)
Low	18	20	12
	(241)	(251)	(34)
	Percentage who contribute $4 or more per week to their church		
Catholics			
Orthodoxy Index			
High	27	45	*
	(150)	(122)	(4)
Medium	16	18	*
	(48)	(56)	(4)
Low	7	21	*
	(30)	(28)	(1)

* Too few cases for a stable percentage.

regardless of his level of orthodoxy.[7] The best contributors are those with unwavering orthodoxy, who reject the religious importance of loving their neighbors or doing good for others. A similar relationship exists among Roman Catholics, the higher the score

[7] The one exception to this generalization occurs among Protestants who are low on both ethicalism and orthodoxy. However, the relatively small number of cases on which the percentage is based makes it difficult to know whether or not to take it seriously. In any event it is of minor interest.

Table 72

ORTHODOXY, ETHICALISM, AND CHURCH ATTENDANCE
(*Church-Member Sample*)

	Ethicalism Index		
	High	Medium	Low
	Percentage who attend church every week		
Protestants			
Orthodoxy Index			
High	55	58	67
	(328)	(247)	(113)
Medium	29	31	52
	(347)	(331)	(44)
Low	19	22	10
	(255)	(165)	(39)
Catholics			
Orthodoxy Index			
High	82	82	*
	(161)	(124)	(4)
Medium	65	60	*
	(51)	(57)	(4)
Low	30	27	*
	(30)	(30)	(2)

* Too few cases for a stable percentage.

on the ethicalism index the less likely a parishioner is to give money to the church regardless of orthodoxy. At the present moment, member commitment to Christian ethics seems to cost the churches money.

Table 72 shows the joint impact of ethicalism and orthodoxy on church attendance. Here again among Protestants it is clear that the higher their ethicalism the less likely they are to attend church regularly. The best attenders are the highly orthodox who reject ethical tenets. Among Roman Catholics it is unclear from these data whether or not ethicalism has any effect at all upon church attendance.

These findings were rechecked within liberal, moderate, and conservative Protestant groups, and within specific denominations as well. In all cases a concern with ethics tended to be incompatible with church attendance and contributions. Furthermore, these same relationships were observed for participation in church organizations and activities.[8]

These findings strongly suggest that the churches are presently failing to engage the ethical impulses of their members: regardless of whether or not they have retained orthodox religious views, to the extent that persons have accepted the ethical preachments of Christianity they seem inclined to treat the church as irrelevant. Obviously, this bodes ill for the future of the churches. It means, in effect, that the churches have yet to find a substitute for orthodoxy which will guarantee their organizational survival. While some form of ethicalism might provide a theological substitute for orthodoxy, the present efforts along these lines have not succeeded.

Sooner or later the churches will have to face these facts. This will require a forthright admission that orthodoxy is dead and, more important, a refusal to compromise with orthodoxy either theologically or institutionally. But it will also require (and here perhaps is the impediment) a clear articulation of an alternative theology, ethically-based or otherwise, and radical changes in forms of worship, programs, and organization to make them consistent and relevant with this new theology.

But even successfully fulfilling these tasks would not insure the survival of the churches. Indeed, the immediate effect would almost certainly be to alienate those members committed to old-time orthodoxy and thus sharply reduce the base of support on which the churches presently depend.[9] The gamble would be that these people could be replaced by renewing the commitment of those members whose interest in the church is presently waning, and by winning new adherents from the unchurched.

Such a radical change of posture is clearly not a present prospect for the more conservative churches. The impact of modern-

---

[8] Nor did controls for social class alter the findings.

[9] See the discussion in Charles Y. Glock, Benjamin B. Ringer, and Earl Babbie, *To Comfort and To Challenge* (Berkeley and Los Angeles: University of California Press, 1967), esp. ch. 9.

ized theology on these bodies has so far been indirect, in the loss of members who change to more liberal denominations. To the extent that these losses remain endurable, and the clergy and laymen remain relatively impervious to modernism they can delay their crisis. Thus if institutional reforms are to come, obviously the liberal churches must lead the way. The data suggest that not only are the liberal churches in the best position to make such changes, but their existence may well depend on it.

At the present time the liberal bodies are functioning as way stations for those who are moving away from orthodoxy, and who are as yet unwilling to move outside the churches entirely. But this influx of new members may prove only a passing phenomenon unless the liberal churches can find a way to keep them and activate them. Their current practices are clearly unequal to this task. For it is the liberal churches who are currently in the poorest organizational health. As can be seen in Table 73 in contrast to conservative denominations, the majority of members of liberal bodies are dormant Christians. They have adopted the theology of the new reformation, but at the same time they have stopped attending church, stopped participating in church activities, stopped contributing funds, stopped praying, and are uninformed about religion. Furthermore, only a minority of members of the liberal bodies feel that their religious perspective provides them with the answers to the meaning and purpose of life, while the overwhelming majority of conservatives feel theirs does supply the answers. Finally, the liberal congregations resemble theater audiences, their members are mainly strangers to one another, while conservative congregations resemble primary groups, united by widespread bonds of personal friendships.

In the light of these data the liberal churches do not seem organizationally sound by comparison with the conservatives.

Although all these signs point to the need for a radical break with traditional forms in the liberal churches, it seems quite unlikely that they will do any such thing, at least in the immediate future. For one thing there is no sign that the leaders of these bodies recognize the situation that confronts them. Here and there one hears a voice raised within the clergy, but such spokes-

Table 73

DENOMINATIONAL PATTERNS OF RELIGIOUS COMMITMENT (Church-Member Sample)

	Members of liberal Protestant churches [a]	Members of moderate Protestant churches [b]	Members of conservative Protestant churches [c]	Members of Roman Catholic parishes
	(982)	(894)	(450)	(545)
Percentage high on Orthodoxy	11	33	81	61
Percentage high on Ritual Involvement	30	45	75	46
Percentage high on Devotionalism	42	51	78	65
Percentage high on Religious Experience	43	57	89	58
Percentage high on Religious Knowledge	17	25	55	5
Percentage who feel their religious perspective provides them with the answers to the meaning and purpose of life	43	57	84	68
Percentage who attend church weekly	25	32	68	70
Percentage who have 3 or more of their 5 best friends in their congregation	22	26	54	36
Percentage who contribute $7.50 or more per week to their church	18	30	50	6

[a] Congregationalists, Methodists, Episcopalians.
[b] Disciples of Christ, Presbyterians, American Lutherans, American Baptists.
[c] Missouri Synod Lutherans, Southern Baptists, Sects.

men are a minority with little power to lead. However, leadership is not the only thing that is lacking. There is no clearly formulated theological and institutional alternative to provide the blueprint for renovating the churches. The critical attack on orthodoxy seems a success, but now what? The new theologians have developed no consensus on what it is they want people to believe, or what kind of a church they want to erect.

What we anticipate is that all of the churches (liberal, moderate and conservative; Catholic and Protestant) will continue a policy of drift, with a rhetoric of hope, and a reality of business as usual. There will be more mergers and more efforts to modernize classical interpretations of the faith, but these will go forward as compromises rather than as breaks with the past. Perhaps more radical change will come eventually, when the trends we see have caused greater havoc, for institutions, like people, have a strong will to survive. Still, institutions do die, and often salvage efforts come too late.

Only time will reveal the eventual destiny of Christianity. As matters now stand we can see little long-term future for the church as we know it. A remnant church can be expected to last for a long time if only to provide the psychic comforts which are currently dispensed by orthodoxy. However, eventually substitutes for even this function are likely to emerge leaving churches of the present form with no effective rationale for existing.

This is hardly to suggest that religion itself will die. Clearly, so long as questions of ultimate meaning persist, and so long as the human spirit strives to transcend itself, the religious quest will remain alive. But whether or not the religion of the future is in any sense Christian remains to be seen. Clearly it will not be if one means by Christian the orthodoxy of the past and the institutional structures built upon that theology. But if one can conceive of Christianity as a continuity in a search for ethics, and a retention of certain traditions of language and ritual, then perhaps Christianity will remain alive.

The institutional shape of the religion of the future is as difficult to predict as its theological content. Conceivably it may take on a public character, as suggested recently by Robert Bellah, or the invisible form anticipated by Thomas Luckmann. Or it may live on in a public witness conducted by priests without parishes similar to religions in Asia. Quite possibly, religion in the future will be very different from anything we can now anticipate. The profound portents of what is to come could easily seem trivial and unintelligible today. As Yeats put it:

> And what rough beast, its hour come round at last,
> Slouches towards Bethlehem to be born?